The Price of Freedom

The Story of a Courageous Manila Journalist

by

Mamerta de los Reyes Block

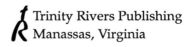

Trinity Rivers Publishing
Manassas, Virginia

Also by Mrs. Mamerta de los Reyes Block

Sulu In Its True Light

DEDICATION

This memoir is graciously dedicated to all the unknown, unsung, unmentioned civilians and warriors, both American and Filipino, who perished so that democracy and justice might be rekindled in the Philippine Islands, especially to those who "disappeared" or were plunged into unmarked and forgotten burial locales.

May their bereaved parents, widows and orphaned children be consoled in that their lives were not lived in vain but had a plan and purpose.

Let the living build on the errors of the past to ensure that there will be a long and just era of peace in their time!

SPECIAL REMEMBRANCE

Everlasting thank you's to the unknown intern-doctor who detected a faint heartbeat in my almost-lifeless body, to the surgeon who operated, Sister Ann(e) and the other nuns of the "Belgian Convent" in Manila, Philippines, who literally saved and gave me the opportunity to live again.

ACKNOWLEDGMENTS

A special grace to all my countrymen who shared their food and shelter when I had none as a wandering refugee.

Many thanks to the farmer whose horse I commandeered to search for refugees in Tarlac Province.

Abounding gratitude to my parents and La Consolacion Convent for demonstrating a way of life for young ladies of my generation as well as succeeding generations.

Again, benedictions to Sister Ann(e) and the religious at the "Belgian Nunnery" for providing hospice to an unconscious and dying prisoner of war.

Special recognition to my daughter, Aida, for endless hours of manuscript typing and suggestions.

To my husband for encouragement and editorial assistance.

To Nestor Mata, my daughter Betty and other members of the family who provided the incentive to forge ahead on a daily basis under starvation conditions — my undying gratitude and appreciation.

A few dates may not be clear-cut due to faulty memory and passage of time. Also, most American names are usually spelled phonetically, as heard by the Filipino ear, in times of wartime stress.

Thanks to the libraries of the National Press Club of Washington, D.C., and the City of Alexandria, Virginia.

FOR USE OF PHOTOGRAPHS:

Thanks to Nestor Mata and Philippine Publishers, Inc.; *Philippine Sea Frontier,* 1945 Christmas Souvenir, Map of Manila for photographs of Christmas in Manila–1945; and the U.S. Office of the American Battle Monuments Commission in Washington, D.C.

Programme of First Annual Convention Manila Chapter, Philippine Legion, 22 February, 1948.

The Manila Chronicle, December 19, 1948; *Times-Herald,* Washington, D.C., September 17, 1951.

Maps on pages xii, 14, 64, by Mr. N. Steven Gordy.

TABLE OF CONTENTS

PERSONNAE

ANTIPORDA, Faustino A.   Major. Fearless guerrilla leader in Rizal Province. Maya Island was a refuge for soldiers and their families. Compassionate.

AYRES, Lew   Movie actor. Assigned to Special Services of GHQ, General MacArthur's Headquarters.

BARILEA, Dominador   Colonel. Founder and Commander of Barrion's Division. Scion of family sugar plantation in Negros Occidental Province. Outstanding personality of resistance movement in Luzon Island.

BLANCO, Pedro   Political visionary. Editor of *The Commonwealth Advocate* and leader of movement for dominion status for Philippines with the United States.

BORJA, Horacio   Attorney, associate of the legendary Dewitt, Perkins, & Ponce Enrile legal offices in Manila. His wife and two children sustained author and other guerrillas during the Occupation. Opened home for first U.S.O.-Filipino style.

CARLISLE, John   Major. Officer-in-Charge of PCAU-4 (Philippine Civilian Affairs Unit) during Lingayen Gulf invasion. Native of Pennsylvania.

CARROLL, Earl   Hollywood personality. Assigned to Special Services, GHQ in Manila.

CLARK, Glenn, Dr.   Multiple book author. College professor, athletic coach, Macalester College, Founder of Camps Farthest Out. Inspirational speaker. Nationally known.

CONNER, H.C., Jr.   Second Lieutenant, Regular Army. 27th Bomb GP(L) – (0-429144). Guerrilla organizer. Native of Kentucky.

DEL FIERRO, Vicente   Free-wheeling editor, *The Star Reporter*, Manila. Courageously exposed anomalous activities of post-war Manila.

LACSON, Arsenio   "Hands-on" Mayor of Manila. Former pugilist.

LANSDALE, Edward   Major. Leader of pacification programs in the Philippines and Viet Nam. Later promoted to Major General, U.S. Army.

LAUBACH, Frank   Internationally acclaimed founder of Laubach Literacy International (LLI) – "Each One, Teach One" program working with grassroots literacy groups. Former missionary-educator in Philippines; Board member of House On Nineteenth Street in Washington, D.C.; author – of numerous books.

LAUDICO, Minerva   Sole surviving leader of Philippine Women's Association campaign bringing suffrage to women in the Philippines. Renowned social worker. Member, House of Representatives.

LIM, Vicente, General   First Filipino to graduate from West Point Academy (1914). Guerrilla leader – captured by Japanese and "disappeared" in Ft. Santiago torture prison.

MACAM, Benigno, Col.   Remarkable charismatic guerrilla leader in Luzon Island. Board member of Philippine Veterans Legion.

MAGSAYSAY, Ramon   Colonel. Founder and organizer of Zambales Province guerrilla division bearing his name. Congressman, Secretary of Defense and President of the Philippine Islands.

MATA, Nestor   Widely acclaimed political columnist. Only survivor of Magsaysay presidential plane crash in 1957. Editor of daily newspaper and various nationally known weekly and monthly magazines. Author of several books.

PAMINTUAN, Mario   Colonel. Leader of large guerrilla regiment adjacent Clark Field Air Base. The Northwest Pampanga Military District (NWPMD) members were indefatigable fighters.

PRINCESS Urduja   Pen name of author. Columnist and publisher of *The Commonwealth Advocate* with the de los Reyes Family. Author of *Sulu In Its True Light*.

QUEZON, Manuel   Mercurial leader and first President of the Commonwealth of the Philippines. Wife, Aurora, outstanding clubwoman and leader of social services for the nation.

QUIRINO, Elpidio   Senator and President of the Philippine Islands.

RAMSEY, Edwin P.   Lieutenant Colonel, Regular Army 2nd Cav. (PS). Guerrilla commander of ECLGA (East and Central Luzon Guerrilla Area).

ROSS, Lanny   Major. Well-known Hollywood cinema singing star. Attached to Special Services of General HQ, Manila.

ROXAS, Manuel   Economist, Lawyer, Senator and Senate President. President of the Philippine Islands at independence in 1946.

SHUBERT, George   Captain. Stationed in Manila, GHQ, General MacArthur's Headquarters. Native of New York.

THORP, Claude A.   Lieutenant Colonel, Regular U.S. Army. Murdered by Japanese for guerrilla activities.

TYDINGS, Millard E.   Long-time Maryland Senator. Co-author of the Tydings-McDuffie Act pledging independence to the Philippine Islands in 1946.

VIZCAYA, Jose   General. Guerrilla resistance army leader in Luzon Island. Charismatic leader of men.

"With malice toward none; with charity for all;
with firmness in the right as God gives us to see the right,
let us strive on to finish the work we are in;
to bind up the nation's wounds; to care for him who shall
have borne the battle, and for his widow, and his orphan—
to do all which may achieve and cherish a just, and a lasting
peace, among ourselves, and with all nations."

Abraham Lincoln
Second Inaugural Address
March 4, 1865

"El amor—
Todo lo sufre,
Todo lo cree,
Todo lo espera,
Todo lo soporta,
El amor nunca deja de ser

Y ahora permanecen la fe,
La esperanza y el amor,
Estos tres;
Pero el mayor de ellos
Es el amor."

San Pablo
I Corintios 13
(Version Reina-Valera)

THE PHILIPPINES

BABUYAN
ISLANDS

Lingayen Gulf

LUZON
• Baguio

South China Sea

• Tarlac

Manila

Philippine Sea

Bataan

Lubang

CATANDUANES

MINDORO

CALAMIAN
GROUP

MASBATE

PANAY

CEBU

SAMAR

LEYTE

PALAWAN

NEGROS

BOHOL

Sulu Sea

MINDANAO

Davao

Zamboanga

BASILAN

JOLO

Celebes Sea

Chapter 1

PEARL HARBOR DAY IN THE PHILIPPINES

Twenty-four hours after the attack on Pearl Harbor, on December 7, 1941, the Japanese Air Force dropped its bombs on Baguio and Tuguegarao and later demolished Nichols and Nielsen fields, U.S. Army Air Force bases on the outskirts of Manila. Hearing a continuous bombardment and feeling convulsing quakes, I ran outside the door of our home and stared with disbelief as I observed that civilian homes surrounding both bases had exploded and were burning fiercely. Black, sooty rolls of smoke ascended almost to the clouds. Panic and pandemonium was everywhere. People were screaming and running in circles as they sought aid for their wounded. My home, less than a mile beyond the perimeter of destruction, survived the initial assault.

As December 8th progressed (being west of the International Date Line, it is one day later in the Philippines than in Hawaii), the grim surprises increased. The radar warning station at Iba, Zambales, about eighty miles northwest of Manila, was obliterated. Continuing the attack, the Japanese Air Force completely destroyed the U.S. airbase at Clark Field in Angeles, Pampanga. Iba was a specially grievous loss since the combined American-Filipino forces now had only one radar station remaining in the entire Philippine archipelago.

On December 10, 1941, I watched from my twelfth-floor office window in the Heacock Building on the Escolta as more than one hundred Japanese warplanes devastated the Cavite Naval Base, eight miles south of Manila.

In a very short time, the U.S. and the Philippines, lost practically all their air power and were left with a severely crippled navy. It was almost a duplication of the pattern of sudden destruction in Pearl Harbor, Hawaii.

However, in this case, the Philippines could never recover from the initial catastrophes.

In order to save Manila from further damage and destruction, the government decided to declare it an open city, remove its troops and not defend it. Soon the Manila newspapers proclaimed in bold headlines, MANILA NOW DECLARED AN OPEN CITY.

Nevertheless, the Japanese dismissed this as an unilateral action and continued to bomb us. Nobody, it seemed, was really prepared at that time for the next Japanese attack that was so imminent. The major Japanese land invasion was unleashed on December 22, 1941, at Lingayen Gulf, in Central Luzon.

However, the American Red Cross, in conjunction with an elite group of Philippine and American society women, had recruited volunteers for emergency services seven months prior to the war. They were bolstered in their efforts by *The Commonwealth Advocate*—a nationally known politico-civic monthly magazine owned by my family.

I was among the first group of young marrieds who had volunteered before the invasion and was with the initial cadre that trained first-aiders, nurses' aides, ambulance drivers and semi-professional nutritionists. Suddenly, we were pulled from our classes and put to work amidst the civilian population with only one or two days' notice.

When President Manuel Quezon evacuated to the island fortress of Corregidor, the city of Manila was then abandoned to the enemy on Christmas Eve. Amazingly, large social parties and festive balls of both the armed forces and civilians were being celebrated up to the very last day. Exclusive hotels and clubs simply closed their windows and covered them with air raid drapes, and the drinking and dancing continued unabated!

This type of conduct reminded me of stories I had read about of the final hours of the "unsinkable" ship, the *Titanic*. Even after it was apparent it could not survive its crash with the iceberg, some people continued to dance, drink and hold high-stakes card games.

The Red Cross urged me to coordinate the evacuation of civilians from Manila to the neighboring provinces of Rizal, Laguna and Bulacan. Little did we know at the time that those very spots would be the scene of some of the fiercest fighting. Neither did I suspect that my auto would be sabotaged by a *Makapili,* or Japanese informer, in broad daylight.

After one trip while traveling back to Manila with two companions, I attempted to slow down the car as we were wending our way through a steep mountain curve. Suddenly, the brake pedal sunk all the way to the floor!

On the right were the jagged walls of the mountain and on the left, a precipitous drop of 400 to 500 feet. I was able to depress the gearshift one notch lower. I continuously rammed the right wheels against the stones and rocks on the right. Steadily, I forced the car to decelerate as it careened off the walls of the mountainside. When we finally reached bottom, I succeeded in stopping the car with relative ease by slamming into a retaining structure.

As we wiped our brows, we looked to heaven with gratitude.

When the tow truck brought the car to a garage, the mechanic pointed to where the brake wires had been cut through, obviously an act of sabotage. Never again during that period did I leave my car unprotected or out of my sight when we made our stops.

Notwithstanding, I continued to use my pride and joy–my two-month-old beige 1941 Studebaker-for at least three daily trips to Antipolo, a town about thirty-two miles from Manila. I transported as many women and children as possible to escape the Japanese troops poised to invade Manila.

However, there were losses. One of my best friends and classmates, Felipa Sumilang, daughter of the governor of the province of Tayabas, was killed as she drove a vehicle in her own province. A few others just could not take the pressure and anxiety of the roundtrips through danger zones and dropped out of the evacuation effort.

Chapter 2

GOODBYE AUTO AND HOME

These first few days had been chaotic and terrifying. The turmoil increased as hungry and desperate people looted barrio stores and the downtown shopping areas.

Our apprehension was rightly founded.

In the middle of the evacuating throngs, a Japanese officer and his aide forced me to halt my automobile at the corner of a downtown street. They vigorously motioned for me to get out of the vehicle with my hands up.

They screamed, *"Kura! Kura! Kura!"* ("Get out of the car!"). They began to withdraw their swords from their scabbards.

There was no possible escape!

They pushed me to the ground. Stepping over my body, they got in the front seats of my car, looked at each other and drove off toward the dockside area.

It was as easy as that! There was nothing I could do to get my car back.

The civilian population was intensely fearful, especially of rampaging low-ranking soldiers with their bayonetted rifles. And the Japanese knew, in turn, that we were deathly afraid of them! They took advantage of that intimidation to induce even more terror.

With tears of anger and frustration blurring my vision, I picked myself up from the street and walked slowly to the sidewalk. "At least I am alive and unwounded," I consoled myself.

After several weeks, some semblance of order was restored.

The Japanese-controlled newspapers and radio stations announced an "All Clear," that it was safe to return. Civilian evacuees rode and walked into the city—to their looted and burned-out homes.

I was not so lucky. As I turned the corner to the street where my house was located, I could not find it. Most of the block looked like a vast construction lot.

Where was my home?

A hole in the ground?

A 6-7-foot deep hole two times the width of my home!

The house that had been my home was now only splattered remnants of a concrete foundation slab. Splinters of wood! A few shreds of clothing!

It must have received a direct hit.

Eduarda, my servant, noticed a shiny circle of metal snagged in the fork of a leafless tree.

She returned my only possession: a broken piece of frying pan blasted from a now-nonexistent cupboard.

It smelled of gunpowder and the fat of *adobo*, vinegar-spiced and broiled chicken.

What a contrast! Two months previously, I had led a caravan of fun-loving couples from "Manila's 400" elite society to my family's country estate on the Pampanga River in Nueva Ecija Province for a pre-Thanksgiving Day picnic and dance.

We had parked our late-model autos next to the blue and pink cabanas bordering the river.

After changing into the modest bathing suits of the day, the men waded through the knee-deep river to a small island. But it was mid-thigh for the ladies as they revealed their feminine curves under the watchful eyes of the chaperones.

A gentle breeze carried the aroma of the barbecue trenches from the shore.

The cooks had labored for twenty-four hours preparing a mouth-watering feast of barbecued piglets (*lechon*), sides of beef and ribs, chicken *adobo*, plus the bounty of the river, especially large Philippine lobsters and jumbo shrimp.

Anchored nearby was a large bamboo raft with a white canopy. On board were two masters of the guitar and two beautiful *violinistas*. They serenaded us continually with popular American show tunes, familiar Spanish favorites, and tangos.

Seemingly, we did not have a care in the world, except for the latest gossip, such as who would be seen with whom at the next dance at Malacanan, the Presidential Palace. Would "Manoling" (President Quezon) dance the tango with them first or with his wife? How many socialites would be flirting as they twirled about during "The Blue Danube Waltz"? Why didn't General MacArthur participate in the dancing? Who would lead the *rigodon de honor,* etc.?

Now, my car was confiscated, my home demolished and all my worldly goods had been obliterated! In that searing realization of such great loss, how incongruous that I wished I could have had at least one barbecued chicken *adobo* wing to eat at that moment.

Thank God, my one-year-old son was alive! He had been visiting with my maid in another part of the city during the air raid. As the two servants studied my face, I held back my tears while I led them down to another locality. Now our only possessions were the clothes we wore!

At this point all I had was my faith in God and the Biblical promise that "I will never leave thee nor forsake thee. I will be with you always."

After walking to the center of Manila, a family friend saw our distress and offered her home and security to my family. This house of concrete and stone was surrounded by a ten-foot wall with a sturdy oak door adorned with a huge brass knocker. It was a grand example of the Spanish fortress manor.

"Now we will be safe," I reasoned.

But, not for very long. Through the "grapevine," I soon learned that the Japanese Imperial Occupational Army was diligently searching for my husband, the editor of *The Commonwealth Advocate,* our family's monthly publication. Of course, as the owner, and a columnist, I was also wanted for questioning by the dreaded *Kempeitai,* or Japanese Intelligence Agency.

And they surely had reason to place us on their "Wanted List." Our glossy, highly successful magazine had been used as an alarm for many years against the expected Japanese invasion and takeover, not only of the Philippines but also all of Southeast Asia. We would now be forever removed! And silenced!

Pedro M. Blanco, Editor, *The Commonwealth Advocate*

Chapter 3

ENEMY "WANTED LIST" = DEATH

For safety and well-being, I hurriedly took my household members to a distant province, Tarlac, intending to leave them there with relatives. When I returned to Manila, I discovered that our magazine editorial offices, equipment and records had been ransacked and confiscated by the Japanese Imperial Army. We learned that my husband, as editor and recently voted Congressman-elect, and I, as columnist, were both on the "Wanted List" and "Declared Enemies" of the Japanese Imperial Government.

The Japanese had been spying on our activities for more than six years. It began in the spring of 1935 when an idealistic entrepreneur, Pedro Blanco, fresh from his studies at Balliol College (Oxford University) returned home to the Philippines. He convinced my family to invest in the publication of *The Commonwealth Advocate,* a monthly magazine. Its purpose was to warn the Philippines to oppose the Tanaka Memorial, Japan's plan to incorporate the Southeastern Asian bloc of nations into Japan's Greater Asia Co-Prosperity Sphere.

The Commonwealth Advocate became a Philippine-American bulwark to alert and inform the nation and had its premier issue in late 1935. My family began a systematic campaign to persuade our country that it was in its best interests to remain as a Commonwealth under the United States *beyond* the 1946 Independence Act as was specified in the Tydings-McDuffie Act of the 1934 U.S.

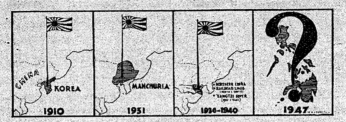

CURRENT HISTORY IN MAPS

KOREA 1910 | MANCHURIA 1951 | 1936-1940 | 1947

Aims and Objectives of The Commonwealth Association, Inc.

Incorporated & Registered under the laws of the Philippines, June 26, 1936

WE BELIEVE in and crave for the political independence and freedom of the Philippines, but to say that we should abide by the Tydings-McDuffie law and accept independence on July 4, 1946, would only mean parting with a senior partner that has proved himself to be fair, generous and kind, for one who will assume the role of a master over us in the same ruthless and despotic manner in which he rules the peoples of the lands over which his flag now flies.

WE BELIEVE that economics cannot be divorced from politics. Hence, the basis of stable economy is political stability. The first problem that the state ought to consider, therefore, should be to secure and maintain a continuous stable government.

WE BELIEVE that neutralization treaties have never been and are not effective guarantees against invasion by imperialistic nations.

WE BELIEVE that the social justice program sponsored by President Quezon can be successfully realized only by a continued favorable trade relations between the Philippines and the United States for a much longer period than that provided for in the Tydings-McDuffie Independence Law.

WE BELIEVE "in good faith that the security, liberty, prosperity, and peace of our common country lie in some kind of political partnership with the United States rather than in complete independence." The only safe way by which this political partnership can be secured and maintained, would be to continue the present Commonwealth government beyond 1946; this partnership to last as long as it remains mutually beneficial and acceptable to both peoples. In other words, WE BELIEVE in the "realistic re-examination" of Philippine–American relations.

BELIEVING AS WE DO in these things we aim to enlist in this cause a million members within two years. This may sound unusually optimistic, but men with faith and conviction, imbued with a sense of responsibility, have wrought miracles. With everyone who believes in our cause doing his duty, we shall and will save these "paradise islands" of ours for ourselves, for posterity, and for DEMOCRACY.

(No fees or dues are necessary to become a member.)

Philippine-American Commonwealth Manifesto

Congress.

By October 1941, our propaganda blitz was supported by newspaper publishers including Mr. Roy Howard of The Scripps-Howard newspapers, famous writers, some U.S. Congressmen, plus senators of the Philippine Congress, executives of the Rodriguez, de la Rama, Mapa families, Judge John Haussermann, mining and merchandise magnates, as well as Paul McNutt, High Commissioner to the Philippines (later Ambassador). President Manuel L. Quezon, taking notice of the important warnings about Japan's territorial ambitions, attempted to strengthen the Philippine Armed Forces and had called General Douglas MacArthur to be the Philippine field marshal in April 1936.

In early November 1941, President Franklin D. Roosevelt sent Mrs. Clare Boothe Luce of *Time-Life* to the Philippines for a fact-finding mission to verify our stand regarding the Japanese menace in Southeast Asia. I personally guided her for three days as she inspected our Army and Navy facilities. (However, she lingered at the bar of the Officers' Club, consuming numerous martinis; eating the olives, she scooped caviar onto a cracker and washed it down with another drink.)

We never knew the results of Mrs. Luce's efforts. We could only assume that it was lost in the Washington diplomatic red tape.

In order to avoid capture and death, we began a life of hide-and-seek with Japanese intelligence officers. My husband and I followed the retreating U.S.-Philippine Armed Forces toward the main defense line in Bataan.

Several weeks later, as I was waiting for a friend on a street corner inside the Philippine Army base of Camp Murphy, a high-ranking American officer stopped his shiny, 1940 Buick red sedan beside me.

"*Senorita!*" he gestured as he got out of the driver's seat. "Here are the keys to my car. They are *yours*! I don't need them anymore! I must report immediately to my regiment on Bataan. It's unsafe for me to drive a car there through the Japanese lines. The car is yours. The papers are inside the glove compartment. *Adios,*

Senorita!"

Before I could finish thanking him, he was already jogging around the corner.

I immediately drove to the home of a relative who worked for the Treasurer of the City of Manila. He changed the registration papers to my name.

What a stroke of good fortune! It was a superb replacement for my recently confiscated 1941 Studebaker.

I continued to use the Buick daily for Red Cross duties. This time I drove only on side streets and back roads.

On December 27th, as I approached Balintawak Monument, north of Manila, I discovered the enemy had set up a roadblock to intercept U.S. Army stragglers attempting to rejoin their units.

It was almost the same scenario as the confiscation of my first auto!

"Kura! Kura!" or ("Get out!") At bayonet point, I was ordered out of the car.

I pleaded with the guards. I showed them the registration papers. The soldiers snatched them from my hand and threw them into the air.

"Kura! Kura!" they screamed. I stepped aside. A Japanese officer got into the car, closed the door and drove it into their compound.

They jabbed their bayonets into the back of my dress and grunted, *"Kura! Kura!"* I quickly moved to the other side of the checkpoint and began the long dusty three-mile walk back to Manila.

Nobody had recognized me!

"Easy come, easy go!" I had heard my American friends say so many times before.

Now—I knew!

On December 31, 1941, we crossed the final bridge leading to Bataan. As we rested a few hours on the Bataan side of the Calumpit Bridge towering over the Pampanga River near San Fernando, we recognized our friend, General Jonathan Wainwright. Our eyes locked several times as we waited. However, during a retreat, no one feels like talking. The next morning, when most of the army had passed over safely, the vital bridge was blown up. We soon went our separate ways and did not see each other again until several years after the war in Washington, D.C.

By January 24th, 1942, the army had fallen back to its final defense line. I remained with my husband as far as the seashore bordering Manila Bay on the Pampanga bayous directly across from the war zone at Hagonoy, Bulacan. Night and day, across the bay we could hear the *Boom—Baroom—Barash* of the ongoing battle on the Bataan side. Fiery artillery tracers were constantly visible, especially at night, lighting up the blackened skies.

And then came the refugees! Thousands of civilian survivors began to land in small boats across the bay next to our location. They required immediate assistance. Already suffering from malaria and dysentery, many were deathly afraid for their lives. An aura of spiritual hopelessness was upon them. Night and day, boatload after boatload of civilians, mostly women and children, landed in a little bayou fishing village called Barrio Consuelo. There were no doctors present, no nurses, . . . and no medicine.

My training with the American Red Cross was finally tested and found to be useful during those early days in 1942! As fast as I could, I tried to help the victims. I made them understand that they needed to proceed to the neighboring hamlets for better medical attention and adequate living conditions.

However, I was wrong!

In village after village, the civilian population had deserted their homes, leaving ghost towns behind them. Everybody was afraid and fleeing for their lives. Any place! Anywhere to escape from the common enemy—the Japanese Army. National hopes were temporarily buoyed by good news from the United States.

We believed President Roosevelt's New Year's Message to President Quezon: "I can assure you that every available vessel is bearing. . . the strength that will eventually crush the enemy and liberate your native land." Chief of Staff George Marshall cabled that "another fifty-five fighters are on the way to join the bombers."

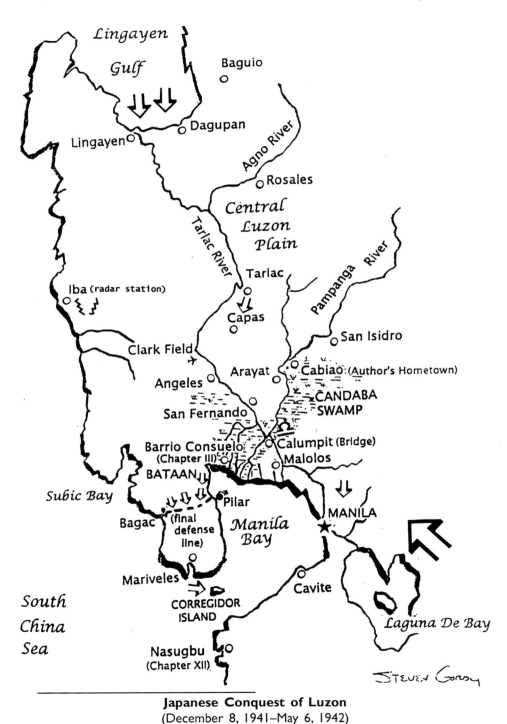

Japanese Conquest of Luzon
(December 8, 1941–May 6, 1942)

We were further cheered by MacArthur's Order of the Day for January 15th. . . . "Help is on the way from the United States. Thousands of troops and hundreds of planes are being dispatched. . . . If we fight, we will win; if we retreat, we will be destroyed."

In a special radio broadcast to the Philippines, President Roosevelt stated, "The resources of the United States, of the British Empire, of the Netherlands East Indies, and of the Chinese Republic have been dedicated by their people to the utter and complete defeat of the Japanese warlords. The entire resources in men and materials of the United States stand behind our pledge."

We still were hopeful despite what our eyes were telling us every day.

Nothing improved; the refugee situation just became worse. By February 1942, many more escapees from Bataan landed here. And by March, we were deluged with additional boatloads of wounded and sick Filipino soldiers. And always, there were mobs of civilians. The thousands became tens of thousands.

As a reporter, my husband, questioned them closely for details of their escape from Bataan. But before we could hear their lengthy explanations, another boatload of sick and wounded would arrive and brush them aside. Every minute counted as we gave them emergency first aid with our limited supplies and encouraged them in every way possible. My only assistants were a brave, local couple who had remained and had compassion for their fellow countrymen.

A few straggler fishermen and farmers provided us daily with small amounts of rice and fish. Occasionally, a local fish pond guard also assisted and showed us the estuary shortcuts inside the bayous.

On March 12, 1942, my husband left in the predawn darkness to cross over to the Bataan war zone with a young soldier who had recently escaped from Manila. I advised him not to go because the two did not know where they would land, or whether they would be killed in the confusion of the battlefield.

He replied, "Honey, the unknown doesn't frighten me. You can manage the situation here. But it is my duty as a journalist to know the real situation there."

I clearly remember my response, "Better a living coward than a dead hero."

He quickly countered, "A dead hero lives forever!"

"But," I answered, "what about us and our unborn child? I'm already three months pregnant." Silence! Then he vanished into the shadows.

One day, as I leaned against a palm tree to steady myself and wipe the perspiration from my eyes, I suddenly remembered my son and his nanny. All I could do as a mother was to pray for peace of heart and to know that he was well-fed, cared for by my relatives and remained far from this tragic scene. Then I wiped away not only perspiration but also my tears of sorrow mixed with tears of hope.

Soon, we lost all count of the days and nights. We just stumbled on daily, doing what we could with what little we had.

But one bright, sizzling hot day, all became quiet and still on the Bataan side of the Bay. Later, we heard on a short-wave radio:

"Bataan has fallen."

Major General Edward P. King had surrendered on April 9, 1942!

Less than a month later, May 6, 1942, the armed forces on Corregidor Island, commanded by General Jonathan M. Wainwright, capitulated.

The U.S. and the Philippines had lost.

The war was now over, but the sufferings only increased!

Chapter 4

BATAAN DEATH MARCH

As we returned to the shore and back onto the main highway, I found people standing on both sides of the highway watching thousands of marching, walking, stumbling, struggling Filipino and American soldiers departing from Bataan.

We learned that the men were being herded to a concentration camp in Capas, Tarlac. The march, which later became known as the infamous "Death March," unfolded before our very eyes.

Indeed it was a death march scene! I saw several American and Filipino soldiers being bayoneted less than ten feet from where we stood, because they could hardly walk, much less keep pace with the lines. Hunger and thirst had debilitated them. Even worse, some had filthy battle-wound bandages barely clinging to their sweaty bodies. The torrid sun beat unmercifully upon their bare skin.

Some civilians lined up on the roadside offered cups of water to the soldiers. But the Japanese guards would snatch the cups from their hands and pour the water onto the ground! Many times, the good Samaritans were beaten harshly for their attempts to help the prisoners.

When a prisoner wobbled and staggered and could not keep abreast, the Japanese shot them. They pushed and kicked the bodies aside into the dusty gutters or threw them into the drainage ditches.

We later heard that the townspeople along the road buried every body they could find regardless of the degree of decomposition.

Only after the war was over did we learn the details of this Japanese cruelty to the vanquished and helpless.

―――――――――――――――――――――――――

Chapter 5

THE GATE

In order to avoid detection and possibly being forced into the Death March, we doubled back to the temporary safety of the barrio. Several hours later, a small boat stopped by our hut on the canal shore. A doctor and a nurse disembarked followed by two wounded, limping Filipino soldiers. After the doctor introduced himself and made a cursory inspection, he asked, "How in the world can you do so much with so little?"

My response was simplicity itself, "Little is much when God is in it."

Laughing, he said, "It is really God's miracle."

Then he revealed that he was with the Pampanga General Hospital. He and the others had evacuated to their present position four months previously. Only five miles from our locality, they were separated by an impenetrable jungle and swampy area. It was a remarkable coincidence.

Introducing his companions, he explained, "This is Lieutenant Arsenio Cavertes and Sergeant Domingo. They survived the Death March on Bataan. They escaped the March and walked until they finally stumbled into our impoverished field hospital. Lt. Cavertes mentioned that both of them met your husband last month in Bataan. He'll tell you the story when we have more time. But, meanwhile, now that it is all over, please, will you help us by escorting these two sick soldiers to Manila? They need to be hospitalized.

"We will take over your duties here. You are too worn out.

You've singlehandedly been doing your best. You remind me of a famous nurse of another war—Edith Cavell."

I did not know who or what he was talking about and was too exhausted to even respond.

As soon as possible, I escorted the two soldiers in a *banca* (native canoe) to Hagonoy by the Bay. Both men were soon overcome in the throes of a malarial seizure. When we docked at the first house we saw in Hagonoy, the residents invited us in when they saw how seriously ill the soldiers had been stricken with malaria.

But, no doctor could be located in the town. Neither was there a pharmacy anywhere for medicine of any kind. Fortunately, the lady of the house had secreted a few quinine tablets behind a wall partition. Thank the Lord she had been saving them! She promptly gave two tablets to each man with a soothing cup of hot tea. Lieutenant Cavertes soon slept through his illness.

However, the sergeant almost died that afternoon. His fever had gone to the tip of the thermometer. There was very little that we could do. As a last resort, we tried using a wet blanket as a hot compress around his body. Finally, after three hours, he fell asleep.

Suddenly, he sat bolt upright on the bed and shouted, "I saw Mr. Blanco go through the Gate!"

"The Gate! What Gate?" I asked him.

This is the story he told us: "Lt. Cavertes and I met Mr. Blanco, your husband, when he first landed on the Bataan shore. He was immediately arrested by the military police. The lieutenant and I were assigned as guards to watch him. His newspaper credentials checked out and later, that morning, he was cleared and released. We became friends for the few remaining days before the final onslaught. Soon after the surrender, the civilian press corps representatives were separated from the servicemen. We saw him no more."

He suddenly stopped and asked for a drink of water. We noticed that his fever was gone.

After three or four sips, he continued, "But, a while ago, I dreamed that the lieutenant and I saw, or I believed I saw, that all of us, including Mr. Blanco, were marching together in a very long line. We arrived at a Gate where each one was checked by a tall white Gatekeeper. Lt. Cavertes was first. He was told he could not go through. I was next in line. I followed him. The Gatekeeper checked me and said, "No!" I stood aside. Then Mr. Blanco went to the entrance. The Man-in-Charge nodded for him to enter. He waved goodbye! And that's when I screamed myself awake. It was all so real!"

Thinking that it was only a malarial dream, I posed a test question to him, "How was Mr. Blanco dressed? Did you see the color of his slacks? Did he wear a hat?"

Without any hesitation, Sergeant Domingo added, "He was wearing beige slacks with long candy stripes. He had on a beige straw hat."

I was almost in shock. It was a perfect description of the clothes he had worn when he had slipped away to Bataan.

Somehow or other, I *knew* then that I would *never* see my husband alive on this earth again!

The next day, our gracious host and hostess procured a small old vehicle—at their own expense. She instructed the driver to take my patients to San Lazaro Hospital in Manila. After a hazardous journey evading Japanese sniper fire, we arrived at the hospital. The sergeant was admitted immediately. However, the lieutenant refused admission, stating that he'd rather go to his own home and take his chances on surviving undetected. I agreed and dropped him off at a relative of my husband's who probably could assist him further.

Chapter 6

WHERE IS MY HUSBAND?

But, "Where is my husband?"

Why had he not escaped from the Bataan Death March in the direction of the fish ponds where the other survivors had gone? I reasoned that perhaps he had arrived there after I had departed for Manila.

"Maybe, if I went back," I decided, "I could find him among the refugee-survivors." I returned to Barrio Consuelo with the help of his cousin, the Treasurer of the City of Manila, who lent me an auto and driver for the search mission to Hagonoy.

When we reached our destination, we observed from the center of the town, and outward all the way to the barrio, that the little fish pond hamlet now was mostly emptied of refugees. A fish-pond guard remarked that the government agents had relocated all the people elsewhere. He didn't know where my husband was. "But, do what you can," he advised. "Look around the seashore. There are many bodies floating onto the beach. Maybe he is one of them."

Frantically, I hired a *banca* (native canoe) and two oarsmen to paddle us to the Bay to look for my husband. We saw and then overturned dozens of bodies. All were bloated and floating face down, gently moving with the tide to the beach. He was not among them!

After several hot, gruesome hours, we returned to Hagonoy. Finally, we began the journey back to Manila.

Several days later, I decided to return to Tarlac Province where the remaining members of my family were being taken care of in safety—I hoped. But, I was able to arrange transportation only to the suburbs of the next town after Manila. Like so many other refugees, I trudged through the red dust and the oppressive heat. Occasionally, I was able to hitchhike for a few miles. Then, I continued my trek through the dust. At night, I slept exhausted, leaning against a coconut tree or on the steps of the local municipal building with other refugees.

After two days of continuous walking, I arrived in Paniqui, Tarlac, on the afternoon of May 11th. It was my birthday!

When I arrived at the Evangelista residence, Dr. J. Evangelista himself greeted me at the door. He was the Director of Public Health for the Province of Tarlac, and my nephew-in-law. From the moment he opened the door and began to cry, I knew that tragedy was near. He told me, through much sobbing, that my husband died on May 6th and was buried two days later in the cemetery outside of the town.

Since my husband was high on the Japanese "Wanted List," he was buried in an unmarked grave so as not to arouse any suspicion. It was a difficult, but necessary, decision to keep the rest of the family from being executed.

Dr. Evangelista filled in the details of my husband's odyssey. Although he had escaped from the Death March, he was suffering from acute malaria and dysentery. He had walked all the way without any medication. In the entire city of Paniqui, there was neither a drop of medicine nor one small pill to sustain him. The town was practically deserted. In Dr. Evangelista's medical opinion "during the long journey without medication he had become severely dehydrated and drained of all his strength. It was a hopeless situation."

Dr. Evangelista repeated his dying words to me: "My wife in Consuelo! My wife in Consuelo!" However, the doctor confessed he did not understand what he was endeavoring to say.

My reaction was that of shock, pain, sorrow. I questioned why God had visited these things upon me. There was no immediate or apparent answer. Looking out the parlor window through tear-filled eyes, I saw only the leaves of the guava trees in the orchard swaying gently in the breeze. The sun's rays beat down heavily upon the world as I could see and feel it. Seated in the living room with grieving family and relatives, I fell to the floor unconscious. It seemed that I was transported back to my father's home following the loss of my beloved mother. He had quoted passages from *The New Testament* to console the family: "Have mercy upon me, O God, according to thy lovingkindness, according unto the multitude of thy tender mercies," and "Blessed be God, even the Father of Jesus Christ, The Father of all mercies and the God of all comfort, who comforts us in all our tribulations."

When I regained consciousness, all the relatives breathed a sigh of relief. I shared my experience in Bataan with them. We cried together. Then there was a hush throughout the room. As I stared out the window again, the shimmering of the guava leaves ceased; all was now quiet in the orchard. I was no longer in tears; a strange peace seemed to flood my inner being.

Since nobody had extra clothing of any kind, I did not follow the custom of "wearing black" as a widow. The great expectations of my husband as a newly elected Congressman from Tarlac Province were now forever silenced under the soil of his home district.

I fell into a deep depression soon thereafter. For almost four weeks, I continued to console myself as I walked daily along the wooden ties of a deserted railroad track for several miles to the next hamlet and then returned. I didn't realize it at the time, but it was part of my grieving therapy on the road to recovery. Neither can I count how many long, lonely hours I spent playing solitaire. I played the cards until they were almost worn out. I never won even one game! But, more importantly, my tension was being relieved slowly as I placed the cards down one by one in their proper order and category.

And after the first few weeks, I recuperated sufficiently so that I did not throw my body across the railroad tracks and beg God for a train to run over me!

Colonel Dominador Z. Barilea
Commander of Barrion's Division
(USAFFE—U.S. Armed Forces of the Far East)

Chapter 7

JOINING THE UNDERGROUND RESISTANCE MOVEMENT

I endeavored to join the newly organized underground forces—Barrion's Division. Its commander, Colonel Dominador Barilea, Chief Paymaster of the Philippine Army, was a friend of my late husband. However, Colonel Barilea rejected my initial attempts to enlist. He ridiculed my efforts as a caricature of a decadent social butterfly and that I could not live up to my editorial *nom de plume* of a dauntless Princess Urduja, the pre-Spanish ruler of Manila.

Pointing to my column on a yellowed page of our monthly magazine, *The Commonwealth Advocate,* he snickered that I was "apt to think that the life of a society girl is nothing but a round of fittings at the dressmaker, pilgrimages to the hair dresser, the manicurist and the masseuse, dances, teas, swimming parties and fashion shows, to be topped with a world cruise."

When he horselaughed, I reminded him, "I've already lost my husband, my home and my business career."

He was not aware that it was physically impossible for me to kill another human being. When I was thirteen years old, I accompanied my father stalking a deer on our rice *hacienda. Tatay* gave me the first shot. I squeezed the trigger. The deer dropped in its tracks as I fell backward from the recoil. After pulling me up, a proud papa walked with me to the fallen deer. As its head turned over ever so slightly in my direction, I observed two tiny nubbins instead of antlers. It was just a fawn!

I gazed into his beautiful soft brown eyes covered with a film of moisture.

Can a deer—*talk*?

His eyes lamented, "I don't deserve this! I only wanted to eat a little grass. Why should I be the one to die? I deserve better than— *this!*"

Now *my* eyes were bathed with moisture.

"*Tatay*, he's so beautiful," I sobbed. "He doesn't deserve to die," I repeated.

I cried and cried and cried.

Papa placed his arms around my heaving shoulders and escorted me to my horse. A manservant accompanied me back to our *hacienda*.

I cried all morning.

I knew then that I could never, ever shoot another living creature, not even my worst enemy—whom I did not have anyhow at that age.

Colonel Barilea noticed my tears but perhaps thought they were the result of my recent bereavement.

He muttered something unintelligible. Then, "With your background and wide political and social contacts, I hereby assign you to G-2, Intelligence Section of Barion's Division, as a Second Lieutenant.

"I'll be in touch with you in less than twenty-four hours."

I was issued neither rifle nor sidearm.

My code name: *bulaklak* or flower. My primary assignment: procuring supplies of food, medicine and pharmaceutical products.

Second, I was to gather and transmit to others the intelligence reports. Through secret connections, I was promptly employed by Menzies & Company, a Swiss drug corporation in Manila. I was to be one of their agents as well as a distributor of medicinal products to pharmacies around the city. I was always garbed in a nurse's uniform to protect my anonymity. The main problem was getting around the city by foot especially since I was in mid-pregnancy.

There was no such thing as a prenatal examination in those times of distress.

What an exciting experience to visit a store, solicit whatever medicinal orders were required, and receive not only an order list but also reports of news for the guerrilla movement! The information or code was always in a sealed envelope so that I would not know the contents. Therefore, if captured by the enemy, I could not reveal classified information. I secreted the notes in my hair or inside my nurse's cap. When I reached headquarters, the notes were subsequently transmitted through the grapevine to the intended recipients.

This new direction in my life began in June 1942. By early August, my superiors commended me as being "very efficient, tight-lipped and wise." Not only did I earn a ten percent commission for my drug orders, I also collected coffee, sugar and medical supplies for the "Family"—our guerrilla unit. The Commanding Officer promoted me to the rank of First Lieutenant.

No matter how careful we were, we could not believe that the Japanese would pay Filipino agents to be traitors and that this deception, in turn, would pay off. But, I thought I had a perfect operational cover that would not create any suspicions.

Again, how wrong I was!

Chapter 8

INSIDE THE JAPANESE TORTURE CHAMBER

I will remember the date forever! On August 4, 1942, as I was exiting the doorway of a pharmacy in Sampaloc, Manila, a Japanese staff car suddenly stopped in front of me. Two soldiers and an officer jumped out, arrested and hustled me off to Fort Santiago Prison. It had formerly served as General MacArthur's headquarters, but after the capture of Manila it became the Japanese headquarters. I was immediately thrown into an underground cell.

My first thoughts were: "How would my family know my whereabouts? How would my landlady know where I was? My . . . *my children*!" I was certain that the underground movement would know soon enough what had happened to its own courier.

Exactly one hour later, I was brought out of my cell for the initial interrogation. At first, things went smoothly and kindly. The Japanese officer in charge came into the room, sat down, brushed his shoes and looked at me. Then, through an interpreter, he queried, "My friend, tell me—you like Japanese? We are here as your friends, yes?"

I was silent.

"We—your liberators. We—Asian Brothers, yes! We free you from Caucasian oppression. See how quickly remove hated British and Dutch! See how easy defeat white Americans! We help—you, yes! You—independent completely—soon. Have new president and government—our kind of people. We—friends, yes!

I thought, "Forty-four years of American rule was now over. Three hundred fifty years of Spanish heritage and religion slipped away.

"Husband gone—dead of acute malaria, home obliterated by Japanese bombs, household servants scattered, both automobiles commandeered by my "Asian friends," family magazine office ransacked, destroyed. Rewarded with a high profile on the "Wanted List" for pro-American activities.

"Can a person or nation that was nurtured in the democratic process, American style, be able to live freely again—or even to survive?"

Then he became more aggressive.

He demanded, "Why are you so loyal to America? Japan love—Philippines. America—no! You are colony. You know Japan want Co-Prosperity Sphere of all Asian countries." He went on and on. Finally he spit out, "Where—your friends hiding? Where—your American leaders, yes?"

I could only shake my head and respond, "I don't know! I am only an agent of medicines and drugstores for Menzies & Company."

He shoved a stack of papers in my face and asserted that this documentation proved I was a guerrilla member helping underground intelligence against the Japanese. He thundered, "You MUST tell the truth and we will let you go home." But, I had nothing to tell him about names and places.

And, I NEVER went home!

Day after day, it was always the same questions: "Where—American leaders of the guerrillas, yes? Where is Balintawak?" I was tortured with inhuman and unbearable pain. All my fingernails were pulled out, one at a time, with a pair of pliers. Force-fed with rotten, putrid-smelling boiled rice. Given the infamous waterhose treatment. Burning cigars were placed on my fingertips. Wherever you were you could hear the screams and groans of those enduring torture. It succeeded in destroying the morale of many an internee.

My cell, which was below the river water level, was flooded almost every night at high tide. I forced my weakened body to crawl to the higher edge of the cell. If I had not, I would have drowned. But, from mid-thigh down, my legs remained in the dark, cold water for many hours at a time. (Perhaps that was the origin of my later arthritis.)

Nobody cared!

My daily schedule never varied.

Monday—torture; Tuesday—torture; Wednesday—torture; Thursday—torture; Friday—torture; Saturday—torture; Sunday—torture! The weeks of torture ground ever so gradually into a month. Pregnancy brought no leniency!

The months passed with unbelievable daily tortures and interrogations that cannot be recorded on paper. September was an especially gruesome month for me. Several other women were also being tortured and given the water treatment and other "tricks of the trade." I recognized Mrs. Josefa Escoda, President of the Philippine National Women's Club, being herded into another torture chamber as I was shoved downward to my underground cell.

I thought, "Why are so many nationally prominent clubwomen being captured and undergoing so much torment?"

Mrs. Escoda and Mrs. Andrea Lim were my mentors in the 1936 women's suffrage campaign, under the auspices of the National Federation of Women's Clubs, to gather 250,000 signatures to petition Congress that women might have the "right to vote."

These two top-echelon clubwomen handpicked a half dozen convent-trained junior and senior high school young ladies to have a prominent role in the program. We were all daughters of the *ilustrados* and wealthy sugar and rice barons.

I personally accompanied the President as we traveled to Iloilo, Negros and Capiz provinces. The other students spoke in major cities and provincial capitals on the island of Luzon. We were housed in the mansions of the fabulously rich clubwomen as we daily led programs and gave speeches on behalf of a Filipino woman's right and privilege to vote in her own country.

Although it took almost a year, we exceeded our goal of 250,000 signatures! Finally, women had won the right to vote in the

Philippine Islands.

Clang-rang! The door to my cell opened!

Clank! It slammed shut! I slumped to the cold, wet floor and my reveries disappeared in the darkened and humid enclosure of my cell.

Then, it was October—the *ninth* month of my pregnancy!

By this time I was no longer able to discern what day it was or what I was doing.

As the nighttime, high-tide river water seeped across my right calf muscle, I hoisted myself up a few more inches. My mind slipped to the stories my father had related to my brothers, sisters, and me regarding his own sacrifices to free the Philippines from Spanish dominion and oppression.

Nueva Ecija, our province, was a hotbed of revolutionary resistance in the late 1890s. Countless men and women were captured, tortured and died for their freedom. When the Spanish militia seized my father, he felt his worst punishment was the *bartolina*. Modeled after the medieval Iron Maiden, *bartolinas* were human-sized wooden or metal boxes with long, sharp knives imbedded in the interior surfaces and walls. If completely tightened, the victim was pierced to death. But the Spanish inquisitor preferred to close them only three-fourths with the prisoner standing at attention. As the person eventually grew weary, the body shifted and he was responsible for his own mutilation.

My father emphasized you could not sit, twist, bend, stretch or even inhale too deeply for more than a fraction of an inch without causing severe wounds and bleeding to death.

Somehow or other, my father survived without divulging any information and was finally released.

He later married, raised a large family, owned a huge rice plantation and was also elected for many terms as mayor of Cabiao, my hometown.

At least there were no *bartolinas* in Fort Santiago Prison. Perhaps, the Americans had destroyed them over the many years of their occupation.

Then the water lapped against my knees, and I pulled my body to the far edge of my cell. I determined that as my father had suffered for freedom and independence that even I, his daughter, was called also to pay a painful price for democracy and freedom for the Philippines and the United States of America.

Mercifully, I fell asleep—to await another day of torture for my country and its ideals of democracy and justice.

I cannot bring myself to describe all the other unspeakable horrors my cellmates and I were subjected to.

What kept me alive was the thought of my child inside me. I had been arrested in the sixth month of pregnancy.

One day, however, as I was being interrogated, I noticed a calendar on the wall of the Japanese torture office. "Horrors," I thought, "is it possibly October? My baby will be due almost any time now—it *is* October!"

And yet another water treatment!

I can barely remember the last interrogation session. Dimly, I heard the officer raising his voice and screaming: "You—hate Americans! You—hate America! You—love Japan!"

Vaguely, I recall placing my hands on my abdomen and with closed eyes I prayed silently to God, whispering, "Lord, help me!"

Everything became black and silent. Then I remembered no more!

Chapter 9

MY BABY LIVES!

First, I heard voices. Then I recognized the sound.

It was the familiar recitation of the Holy Rosary from my childhood. I opened my eyes and looked around me. Upon the ceiling, around the walls—everything was white.

A white wing was bending over me. I thought aloud, "Thank you, Lord! I made it into Heaven." I believed the white wing was the wing of an angel.

Nearby, a voice responded ever so gently, "No, dear, you are still here. You are in the Belgian Mission School. I am Sister Ann."

"And my baby?" I asked.

The white-clad nun pointed at the corner of my room to a small bamboo basket with a white coverlet. It was my baby!

Breathing a sigh of relief, I said, "Thank you," and fell asleep.

The following morning I awakened to the smell of food on a tray. Sister Ann, the Belgian nun, came to the bed and explained what had happened to me.

"Yesterday, about 6:00 P.M., we heard a terrible pounding on the back door of the convent. It was the driver of an ambulance.

"A doctor riding in the ambulance brought you out and rushed you inside saying, 'She will have a baby! We have to hide her! She was a prisoner at Fort Santiago Prison!' That was all the nuns needed to hear. They had hidden so many other guerrillas the past few weeks."

She continued her story: "Yesterday, the ambulance driver picked up three bodies from Fort Santiago. You were one of them.

You were all consigned to the morgue and unmarked graves.

"The intern-doctor was playing with his stethoscope and found the other two prisoners already dead. When he came to your body, he detected a heartbeat and faint signs of life! He determined that the baby inside you also was still alive! The Convent was the nearest place they passed on the road to the morgue. Our doctor performed an emergency Caesarian operation in our infirmary and saved both you and your baby.

"We can't keep you any longer. It's too risky. We'll have to send you somewhere else where it will be safe. So, the doctor who helped you will send some trusted friends to pick you up today." Sister Ann's flowing tears were those of joy and thanksgiving for the miracle of new lives! She also pressed several pills into my hand to help my grossly swollen legs return to a normal size and shape.

Shortly thereafter a police car pulled up to the side door of the Belgian Mission Infirmary. Two husky uniformed police officers rushed to the door and knocked vigorously.

They announced to the nun on duty, "We have orders to pick up your new patient and her baby." She became immediately frightened and desperately sought a way to close the door, fearing I would become a prisoner again.

However, I was able to peek through the partially opened door. From my bed I recognized Officer Francisco Baguisi, my own cousin-in-law! He hurriedly bundled the baby and me and hid us in the back of the police vehicle. He then drove as quickly as possible to his home outside Manila where I could recuperate. I knew that the Japanese trusted him in his Manila police duties.

But only on the trip did he reveal that he was a member of the USAFFE (United States Armed Forces of the Far East)—Barrion's Division of guerrillas.

Chapter 10

I BECOME A NON-PERSON

It was a harrowing and nightmarish experience to realize that now I was for all practical purposes—a non-person!

Every prized item of civilization and accomplishment disintegrated when the enemy bombed my home into oblivion. All personal identification and treasured family mementos and pictures vanished.

What I had labored and sacrificed for during seven years in my business and professional career had been ransacked and destroyed.

My published book, *Sulu In Its True Light*, was burned.

Loose and bound copies of our magazine were confiscated by the Japanese.

Five months after we lost the war, I became a nonentity!

I had "disappeared" into the Ft. Santiago torture prison and the Japanese had consigned my almost lifeless body to an unmarked grave.

To the world at large, if I had really ever lived, I was now—dead!

To this date, only two captionless photographs have surfaced from the first thirty years of my life—showing that I had ever existed.

In addition, I had lost so much weight during my incarceration that only a few of my relatives were even able to recognize me. I changed my hairstyle to a raised, knotted bun and dressed in peasant clothes. I was a complete stranger to most people I encountered in my daily rounds.

My life now became oversimplified. I no longer needed to meet a payroll for printing presses, editorial writers, reporters, clerks, etc.; the Japanese had destroyed my family monthly magazine.*

My driver and his wife became unemployed when the enemy commandeered my new automobile.

There was no use to have two household maids because my home was blown up with one bomb. A laundress was no longer a necessity since I only had one set of clothing.

A cook was not a priority because almost anybody could boil water for rice or a few sweet potatoes.

Only Eduarda from San Narcisco remained as my personal maid and nanny for my children.

It made no difference whether I used my old code name of *bulaklak*, or "flower" or my own name since I had "disappeared" and was declared dead.

However, as soon as I had reasonably recovered my strength from the imprisonment and Caesarian operation, I resumed my underground guerrilla intelligence activities.

This time, I became a rice and sugar merchant.

Retail selling of sugar was not too difficult. Early every morning, the driver of a *caratela*, or horse-drawn cart, would meet me. After we loaded sacks of native brown sugar on it, I would then go from store to store throughout the city and measure it out pound by pound to the individual shopkeepers throughout the sweltering tropical day. When globs and patches of sugar clung and stuck to my uniform, the flies by droves loved to follow my movements. But the worst times occurred when the bees threatened to swarm over me.

"Patience," whispered my conscience. "You are doing all right. It is not in vain today. You gathered some news and supplies to maintain the strength of our movement."

---

* Editorial Assistant "S.P." (Lopez) survived and later became Ambassador to U.N. and U.S.A. in Washington, D.C.

Chapter 11

"ZONA! ZONA!" or JAPANESE STREET JUSTICE

In the latter days of 1943, the Philippines were enduring severe shortages of food supplies to the public market. The puppet president, José Laurel, was attempting to run the government efficiently under Japanese dictatorship. Most of the staple foods were being consumed by the Japanese Army and Navy. There were rumors that the majority of the harvests were being shipped to Japan itself. Neighbors began to share with neighbors what little they had for as long as it lasted.

My retail sugar business was severely crippled when the Japanese rationed me to only one 50-lb. sack of sugar for an entire week! I did not know how long we would be able to survive on the profits of such a small consignment.

One day shortly thereafter, tragedy struck our little business and the life of my son. Taking a short midday break from the routine of sugar distribution, I returned to my second floor apartment in the San Juan suburb of Manila to be with my children. Suddenly we heard the screech of truck brakes. Then the terrifying screams of *"Kura! Kura! Zona! Zona!"* A *zona* is the Japanese Army's maneuver to isolate a neighborhood in an attempt to apprehend suspected pro-American sympathizers.

The ancient doctrines: "man's house is his castle" or sanctity of the home including the right to bear arms to defend yourself have *no validity* when an invading army overruns your beloved country.

It was a time of intense fear, for nobody knew who would be trapped in the tentacles of Japanese cruelty. All Filipinos know when they hear those dreaded words they are about to be threatened, hurt or going to lose their lives very quickly. The guttural *"Kura! Kura!"* shouts increased and became louder. We felt the vibration of feet stomping on the stairwell leading to our apartment. The door was forced open. As the soldiers burst in, we cringed in the corner of the living room. They were searching for young male, pro-American guerrilla sympathizers. Nestor, the eldest male at 14 years of age was the chief suspect—fitting their stereotypical profile.

It was impossible to resist a squad of burly, angry soldiers bearing rifles with fixed bayonets. Chairs, tables, dishes and utensils were thrown to the floor, as Nestor with rifles and bayonets pointing at his back was pushed down the steps. Nestor could not understand what he had done to anger the soldiers. Or, why they really wanted *him*! However, he knew it was a matter of Life and Death! Warning the others to remain, I followed.

As they came to the rear of the truck, another soldier took his bayonet and placed it tightly against the skin of Nestor's neck. He screamed again, *"Kura! Kura!"* or "Stand up straight and get ready to die!"

The streets were obviously empty. Nobody stayed around very long when a truckload of Japanese soldiers drove into your neighborhood or near your house. However, everybody was peering out of the corners of upstairs windows and praying that they, in turn, would not be pulled out of their houses and that, God willing, not too many people would have to be killed before they departed. They could only stand by helplessly and pray.

Nestor, with a rifle at his chest and bayonet at his throat again heard the dreaded *"Kura! Kura!"* Then, a black-hooded civilian lifted himself up from the body of the truck and stared in his direction.

The soldiers nodded and demanded, "He is guerrilla—yes?"

I could not believe the scene that was unfolding in front of my

July 13, 1955

To my friend
Nestor Mata
with affection.

President Magsaysay with presidential reporter, Nestor Mata

eyes. My son—my innocent son—was about to be killed on the street because of this traitorous informer. But, Filipinos had seen this scenario over and over as the Japanese attempted to stamp out the guerrilla movement.

I ran over to the Japanese soldiers, trying to avoid the other ten squad members as best as I could. I screamed and begged them, "He is *only* a boy. He's only 14 years old! The regular *caratela* driver is sick. He is only helping me today. He's a *schoolboy*! He doesn't KNOW any guerrillas! Please! He is innocent! Just look at him!" I was on my knees in the middle of the street near the back of the truck staring into the eyes of the two armed soldiers and the hooded man.

"Please! Dear God! Have mercy on him!" I prayed. Then, I saw a faint flicker of understanding on the face of the Japanese soldier with the poised bayonet. I knew the Lord had answered my prayers, because the informer shook his head from side to side—signifying that he was NOT a guerrilla member! Then the soldiers shouted again, "*Kura! Kura!*" or "Get out of here before it's too late for you!" Accordingly, they let him go. Just like that.

He stumbled and crawled back to the house. I got off the ground, thanking God for answering my prayer so quickly and fully. Did not God say, "Call upon me, and I will answer thee, and show thee great and mighty things which thou knowest not"?

I barricaded the broken door. However, I had to leave the other family members so that we could "earn our daily bread." The horse had remained patiently at his hitching post the entire time. Somehow or other, Nestor* was able to start the *caratela* and move on.

As we left, I saw another dismal, cruel affair unfold. Two Filipino youths who had come down the far side of the street completely unaware of what was happening had been caught in the *Zona*.

At bayonet point the other soldiers pushed them in front of the truck's tailgate.

"He is guerrilla—yes?"

The hooded informant nodded in the affirmative. They were

---

* Later became Presidential correspondent to Philippine White House and award-winning newspaper and magazine editor.

beaten up and thrown roughly into the bottom of the truck—to their doom! The truck then roared toward the far end of the street as we slowly wended our way in the opposite direction in the *caratela*.

The *Zona* was now completed.

But—my daily struggle must continue until sundown.

However, that night was the *end* of my sugar retail business!

Fortunately, I was then given orders from Colonel Barilea to "lay low" for a period of time. Although we returned to the home of Mrs. Borja in the middle of Manila, I still needed to earn money for food.

Quiapo Market was about a block or so away. I would go there daily. From a friend, I would get some second-hand clothes on consignment and sell them, hopefully, for a small commission. My daily net allowed me, if lucky, to earn the money to purchase our *one meal* of the day—a dinner of two or three small sweet potatoes, a cup of rice and perhaps one coconut or a duck egg. This was the main meal for seven in the household. Mrs. Borja, my landlady, saw to it that my babies usually had at least one-half cup of milk for the day.

Chapter 12

A MASSACRE AND A
TRANSMITTER

One week before Christmas 1943, I received a verbal order to proceed to the Barrion Guerrilla Headquarters in the jungles near the foothills of Bulacan and Rizal provinces. When I arrived, I was immediately instructed to dress up in a Japanese Army uniform complete with special cap. My assignment: to be the designated driver for their next sortie. As I walked along a jungle trail, I suddenly saw a Japanese staff vehicle with three officers seated in the back seat. I flinched, but when they saluted Colonel Barilea, I knew that they were also Filipino guerrilleros disguised as Japanese officers. Somehow, they had "liberated" a functioning, very heavy (1940) Buick Japanese staff car with double blue stars. Both sides of the hood were festooned with the two blue flags denoting its power and authority.

No explanation was given me except to wear the Japanese Army uniform with the special cap. I silently thanked God there was no blood on the uniform. The men in the back seat were similarly attired but in high-ranking officers' uniforms. I thought I recognized one of them from Mindanao, but they kept their heads down and maintained silence. Colonel Barilea, who spoke fluent Japanese, sat in the front seat next to the driver. Obviously, the former owners had been "taken care of" and their bodies disposed of in the jungle or deep in an abandoned mine shaft. He gave us disposable cosmetic kits, and we made ourselves up to simulate the

Japanese complexion.

When darkness fell, we left our hiding place and proceeded the seventy-five miles to Nasugbu, Batangas Province. Colonel Barilea, in a staff officer's uniform, gave explicit directions for navigating every twist and turn in the roads.

When we arrived at the rear of the Japanese center, we turned the headlights off. We heard loud music being played in the barracks. We inched our way forward and stopped in a shadowy space. I was ordered to crouch under the steering wheel and to remain invisible. I held the key to the ignition in my right hand—ready to start the car the minute the colonel gave the signal.

It happened so quickly!

In less than two minutes I heard a loud *Bang! Bang!. . . Rat-a-tat-tat. . .* and a heart-stopping *Whizzzzz!* Several minutes later, all was silent. Then orange flames and smoke poured out of the front of the barracks.

I looked up and saw several men scurrying in the shadows toward the car. They were struggling to carry an obviously heavy bundle covered with blankets. As soon as the men and their mystery package were safely in the car, Colonel Barilea gave the command to start the car and to follow his orders. Almost immediately, I understood that the bundle was a priceless radio transmitter! This was monumental! Now, we could both *SEND* and *RECEIVE* messages to other units of guerrilleros as well as to the Americans. Our mission now was to stay alive and remain uncaptured.

I drove the heavy blue Roadmaster Sedan with twin Japanese flags and blue stars in record time. Our destination: back to guerrilla headquarters.

At each of the nineteen Japanese checkpoints, I and my fellow guerrillas held our breath while Colonel Barilea ordered the officers and sentries, in perfect Japanese, to step aside and not to hinder or interfere with our important mission to Manila. The Japanese were subservient and obedient. As they bowed very deeply, not one of them dared to sneak a glance at our vehicle's occupants since they were fully aware of the flags and the significance of the blue stars.

When we finally reached our headquarters, our attempts to enter were almost thwarted by Mrs. Barilea, the colonel's wife. Seeing the uniforms of Japanese officers, she naturally panicked and refused us entrance. The longer our admittance was denied, the more desperate our situation became. If the staff car had been spotted, an immediate investigation might have been ordered. However, the colonel, in desperation, loudly hissed in Tagalog his wife's nickname, *"Mameng"* (for Carmen). Upon recognizing her husband's voice, she admitted us and made the preparations to provide secure hiding places.

After a quick conference, we decided to scatter to remote jungle barrios beyond Polo. By dawn, we were well on our way. The staff car and the uniforms magically disappeared. None of us ever mentioned the incident again until many years after the war.

The physical and, perhaps more importantly, the emotional toll we all shared during this mission was immeasurable. First the guilt of massacring an entire barracks of soldiers within a span of less than ten minutes, coupled with killing a driver and four officers, plus the strain and tension of bluffing our way through nineteen enemy checkpoints most certainly resulted in psychological scars we would all sustain for many years. (The term PTSD—Post-Traumatic Stress Disorder was unknown to us in those days.)

The sneak attack on the Japanese barracks to acquire the radio transmitter was an outstanding coup which no doubt gave us a great advantage during the rest of the Occupation. However, in retaliation, the Japanese declared numerous *zonas* in the area surrounding the barracks, endeavoring to apprehend the perpetrators.

Many innocent civilians were tortured to the point of death in an attempt to force them to give knowledge regarding the events that they were totally unaware of. Sadly, many resistance fighters were captured and suffered the same tragic fate.

All of these brave "unsung heroes" join a long line of patriots who gave their lives to keep the Philippines free. Their rewards did not include medals, backpay, or recognition—only an unmarked, mass grave!

Chapter 13

NEGRITOS AND THEIR GOD

In less than one and a half years, the invading enemy army had reduced my country to starvation level. Most of our staple products of rice, sugar and corn were being confiscated by the Japanese authorities. In Manila, the streets were gradually becoming more and more overrun by beggars and the homeless.

Early one Monday morning, walking along the street near Far Eastern University, I turned a corner and saw an elderly woman sprawled on the street with both arms upraised. She was obviously near death. As I approached she begged, "Put just a little water in my hands so I can drink!" I hurried to the nearest coffee shop, filled a cup of water and brought it to her. I lifted the rim to her lips. She drank only two sips. Then she gave a loud cough and died in front of my eyes.

I was shocked and never forgot the face of that desperate woman, but it was not a too unusual sight or atypical of what was occurring daily on the streets of Manila, especially in the downtown areas.

The only ones who seemed robust or anywhere near approaching normal health were the formerly wealthy and aristocratic men and women who had collaborated with the enemy. It broke my heart to see so many with inherited wealth, who were members of the *ilustrados*, or "high society women," including my former classmates and dear friends, go over to the enemy side so that they could retain their glamorous status. Those who consented to be on intimate terms with the enemy not only did not suffer but actually increased in status and prestige. In fact, some of society's privileged ones became multimillionaires at the expense of their suffering countrymen!

Later that week, my commanding officer, Colonel Barilea, commissioned me to deliver a sealed envelope to an underground organization of soldiers in the northern mountains led by an American officer escapee of the Bataan Death March.

I thoroughly understood that if I were caught there would be neither imprisonment nor torture. This time I would be immediately executed.

I tucked the envelope inside my bosom and began the long trek to the northern Ilocos region.

Never did I dare travel the principal or secondary roads, because I might be trapped in a sudden Japanese *zona* maneuver to isolate a particular district as they searched for undercover activities.

Instead, I walked on gravel and dirt roads that bypassed the major population centers. To the world at large, I was a lonely woman in desperate search of her ex-soldier husband or war-displaced children.

At dusk I slackened my pace on a dirt road near several primitive houses in an outlying barrio or suburb. A mature farm lady inquired, "Good evening, honored pilgrim. Welcome to our humble farm. May I know your name, please?"

According to strict guerrilla intelligence instructions, I responded, "Thank you, *amiga;* I am *bulaklak,* a flower looking for my flower garden."

Immediately assuming that I was completely distraught from wartime disasters and deprivation, she formally invited me to share her home for the evening.

The unwritten law of the rural Philippines requires that no Filipina should *ever* allow another woman, especially a stranger in their community, to remain unattended or unhoused for the night! Somebody must invite them in for a meal and a place to sleep!

Thanking her for the courtesy and trudging behind her, I noticed another farm couple glancing at me.

That stare resulted in my having a restless night at my lodgings.

Early the next morning, addressing me as Flower, they revealed that they were Daisy and Violet and Orchid, and insisted I remain on the back roads. Other "flower people" would assist me in my journey at the next towns.

The following evening after eleven more hours of continuous walking, I entered another hamlet. I was also courteously addressed and inquired of my name. When I explained, "I am a flower searching for my garden in the next town," they also revealed *their* "flower" aliases and invited me to abide at their hut.

That night I could enjoy our shared supper of rice, tomatoes, fish sauce and a boiled duck egg and slept securely.

After breakfast of additional fish sauce with rice and a hot cup of burnt rice coffee with native brown sugar, I resumed my journey toward another village—to await another flower person to greet me.

It was too dangerous to ask questions—until today, so I do not know how Colonel Barilea arranged for fellow patriots to shepherd my pathways. (However, I speculate that our 2-way radio may have played an integral part.)

Upon reaching my destination several days later, I observed an outfit of malnourished, emaciated and sickly soldiers commanded by an American, Captain H. C. Conner, Jr.

They had not eaten for several days. Most were suffering with malaria and dysentery. A few Filipino soldiers were accompanied by their wives and skin-and-bone children.

I delivered the envelope. Inside was a letter of hope and inspiration, emphasizing that the liberation forces were coming soon from the shores of Australia and New Guinea. To prove the point beyond the shadow of a doubt, Colonel Barilea had given me ten American-made cigarettes and some stateside candy to show the new group.

One glance at the Chesterfields, Camels and Lucky Strikes in their shiny white wrappings was proof enough. They puffed slowly and majestically as they shared the cigarettes with each other and compared them with the rough-hewn, brown-wrapped Philippine *cigarillos*. They knew in their hearts that the only way for white cigarettes to be in their hands was through the agency of an American submarine and that soldiers would soon be following.

But what was more important to them than any cigarettes or candy bars was an immediate supply of food and medicine. Or else, they would not be around to celebrate any American victories!

Captain Conner soon asked me, "Well, thank you for these supplies, but can you help bring us some food?"

Not knowing exactly what to respond, I blurted out, "Let us pray that God will send us some."

Everybody laughed aloud at that remark.

When I inquired if anybody wanted to pray for food, most of them mocked me. However, five men did respond from more than one hundred present in that jungle wilderness camp.

We had a very simple prayer asking God to send some food— *pronto!*

One sweaty hour went by. There was no answer to prayer.

Two hours dragged by in that sweltering heat and humidity.

The children began to cry aloud begging their parents for some food. Any food! The men were holding their stomachs and moaning from either hunger or malarial pain.

They taunted that God would not answer our prayers. That all was hopeless!

Suddenly, the duty sentinel on the next hilltop relayed, "Some strange looking men are climbing up a hidden jungle trail. They have baskets on their heads. Looks like they're armed with bows and arrows. They've got primitive javelins in their hands."

The Captain shouted, "Let them come on in. But we'll remain hidden in the depths of the jungle."

Shortly thereafter, emerging from amidst the jungle foliage, we saw five pygmy-type men, or Negritos. These dark-skinned aborigines, less than five feet tall, with kinky hair, were very muscular. They wore only G-strings. Each man carried a crude handmade basket of reeds and grasses on his head.

"*Shhrooop-ah-shreeeeep!*" the Captain whistled. We all emerged from our hiding places. The leader bowed in our direction.

Then they unloaded the baskets, removed the grass covers and showed us the contents.

It was a veritable feast! We saw and smelled the boiled wild rice, fresh corn and roasted native birds. The birds, slightly smaller than pigeons, had been barbecued. The sticks were still protruding from their bodies.

Captain Conner requested me to speak to them.

The aborigines could not speak English.

I attempted to converse with them in Spanish, Tagalog, (the Philippine national language), the Ilocano dialect of that area, as well as Pampango and Visayan. I gave up. It was hopeless. Not even one word was known to them!

I paused for a second, wondering what to say next. In that very moment, I remembered something my father had taught us at daily vespers during my childhood: "If any of you lack wisdom, ask it of Him who giveth liberally and upbraideth not." I thought that if they could not understand spoken language, they could surely understand the universal language of the body, head and hands.

Thus, using my hands, I pointed to the food and then turned my pockets inside out to show that they were empty.

Emphasizing that we had no money to pay them, I shook my head vigorously from side to side in a negative manner.

One of the aborigines then came forward, bowed and shook his head up and down. He spread out his hands in a manner that signified they did not expect any kind of money or payment.

Next, he opened his mouth wide, made chewing motions and pointed his arms and hands toward the sky and sun and clouds and hills, thus indicating that the God Who had made and created those things had told them that there were some hungry people over the next mountain. They, as His servants, were to bring cooked food to them.

We acknowledged God and His gifts through them. We

thanked them profusely. We bowed deeply toward them.

The Captain had a change of heart and now asked me to "say a Blessing," or words of Grace, before we began to eat.

There was no doubt whatsoever in anybody's mind that we were being fed, and well fed at that, through God's everlasting grace.

While we were eating, the Negritos slipped silently away and disappeared into the background of giant leaves and brambles.

_____

Chapter 14

A STRANGE CURE FOR MALARIA

It seemed that this was just the beginning of a week of miracles, or of the unusual, to those who could comprehend it.

The very next afternoon, many of the men and women, as well as the small children, who had malarial fits, became violently ill with spasmodic, deep and uncontrollable malarial shaking spells.

There was no medicine available. So, they suffered.

Again, I invited those who wanted to pray for medicine to become available. Nobody mocked me this time. But only eleven people joined in faithful prayer. They said they now believed in the power of prayer. Well, at least that was slightly more than double the five of the preceding morning who had prayed for food.

Our prayers were again very simple: "Please, dear God, help some medicine to come our way. We are absolutely hopeless. We saw your answer yesterday. Can you help us again this afternoon by doing what is impossible to us but available to you?"

For the second time, a childhood memory came back to my mind, just as it did when we were stranded in Barrio Consuelo during the siege of Bataan. Following the example of my grandmother's memory when she was still alive in my hometown of Cabiao, Nueva Ecija, I suggested to several men that they gather roots, herbs and even the bark from the trees and bring them to me.

We put all of it in large ten-gallon gasoline cans filled with water. Then we let it boil for several hours. When it looked like it was ready, I informed the Commander to begin ladling it to those who were sick.

He took one look at the bubbly-brown concoction with its abominable smell and groaned inwardly.

Captain Conner challenged, "Mamerta, that's a horrible looking mess to drink as medicine. You drink it first! If you do not fall dead, I will let everybody else drink it."

I did not like that idea at all! But with a silent prayer in my mind, I seized a coconut shell cup, scooped a portion of the liquid into it and drank of the worst-tasting, horrible-smelling liquid I had ever known in my life.

I survived five minutes, ten minutes.

At twenty minutes, I was still on my feet.

Then he ordered everyone to partake of the medicinal potion that was even worse than the cod liver and castor oil I had tasted as a child.

Everyone who drank of the bitter, crude-smelling, putrid liquid was healed that very day!

Two months after the Liberation battle, a few of us went back to see what kinds of herbs and barks we had used for medicine. We discovered that several of the trees belonged to the quinine family. The bark and leaves we had scraped and boiled were a potent and effective malarial cure. The other roots we could not identify.

Chapter 15

MISSING IN ACTION—IN CEMENT

Meanwhile, we discovered another active guerrilla band in Rizal Province. Their activities were so bizarre and unusual it was difficult to comprehend what they were accomplishing until you spoke secretly with the leaders or observed the "final solution" in action.

Only Major Faustino Antiporda and a few trusted associates knew the exact number of Japanese enlisted men and especially officers they assisted in becoming A.W.O.L. or *MIA*—Missing in Action. It was a risky maneuver. His men would follow an enemy platoon until they went into narrow streets at night, or were on special missions in the rural zones. They waited until the soldiers divided into squads and then went single file into the dark or deserted areas.

When one, or occasionally two, soldiers lagged behind, his men waited until they turned a corner and then pounced on them when they were alone. They were spirited away in the dark, or else were hidden temporarily in a jungle holding-trap.

They were then quickly transferred to a staging area in another secluded hideout. The majority were transported to the Madrigal Cement Factory. Antiporda's men stripped the victims of all that could be recycled back into the war effort against their own country. Especially needed were rifles, uniforms and personal identifications. Nothing was wasted.

Their corpses were quickly secreted onto the assembly line of the factory during the night shift when nobody was around. In less than fifteen minutes their bodies became a part of the cement dust that was being manufactured. It was later bagged and shipped out for distribution. Nobody in the factory was 100 percent knowledgeable of the entire process except a few trusted managers who were sworn to absolute secrecy.

Therefore, if anybody were caught, he would only be able to testify as to how many Japanese he personally knew that disappeared, or how the regular cement process functioned. With the possible exception of Major Antiporda, until this very day, it is unknown how many scores (or hundreds) of Japanese met their ancestors and are now a part of the vast cement road network of the Philippines. Nor may any man know how many are imbedded in various buildings and other structures cemented in place as a dusty testimony to the agencies and destructions of war.

When a government building in Manila seems to have a golden glint in the sunlight, it is possibly part of a pulverized gold tooth that was not removed because of haste and sudden danger near the factory.

When Major Antiporda applied for his guerrillas to be recognized by the American Recognition Unit of the U.S. Army, the young clerk-officers could not comprehend or begin to understand how much they had sacrificed for the Americans. The story was so gruesome that it was rejected as unbelievable.

Only much later, when the terrors of the Holocaust were revealed, would some people believe Antiporda's story.

Until the day he died, Major Antiporda hoped that some sort of American recognition would be given to his men. They were not asking for "backpay money"—only acknowledgment that they had served and had helped to shorten the war in their own little area.

Several years later, Antiporda was finally recognized as a Staff Sergeant for three months and as a major for two months: a total of five months actual army participation instead of the three years he fearlessly served.

Chapter 16

SURVIVAL UNDER WATER

Colonel Barilea delegated me as a courier to bring a secret message to another guerrilla camp in the town of Meycauayan, Bulacan. Meycauayan, the center for leathermaking on Luzon, was noted for its horribly polluted orange-red river coursing through the town. The river and buildings reeked with the fumes from various chemicals used in the tanning process. When you were still several miles away, you knew you were approaching the town because of the overwhelming odor.

Delivering the message to Colonel Santos of Bulacan was no big problem. However, when I was ready to depart for the return trip to Manila, we saw a rolling cloud of dust on the narrow road leading to our rendezvous house. A Japanese staff car with an officer and two soldiers was rapidly approaching. Colonel Santos was in double jeopardy inasmuch as he was also the town mayor and considered by the Japanese as being "friendly."

He immediately ordered me to go through the back door of the house and run to the banks of the river to warn the two Americans there to flee for their lives.

His plan was to upend a *banca*, or native canoe, and shove it seven to eight feet from shore to provide a hiding place for the Americans. On the farther side was a pathway almost surrounded by water. The Americans were to submerge themselves on the far side of the *banca* and breathe through the two long bamboo tubes he miraculously pulled from a desk drawer.

Hastily, he pushed the brown tubes into my hands and

screamed, "Tell the two Americans to submerge themselves and breathe through these tubes!"

I scooted as fast as I could to the bank where the Americans were hiding and explained the plan to them. They reacted with shock and amazement, but quickly realized that the alternative could prove to be horrendous—possible capture, torture, and worst of all, execution and being dumped into an unmarked grave.

As I pointed out the direction to them, they had already out-distanced me and were on the other side of the *banca*. By the time I reached the shoreline, they had already submerged, and their two bamboo tubes could not be distinguished from the hundreds of other weeds and vegetation in the river.

The Japanese had been "tipped off" by an informer that several *canos*, or white-faced Americans, were near the house. They had sped down the road to capture them.

As I returned to the farmhouse, I saw the two Japanese soldiers running toward me. I heard the "Plack! Plack! Plack!" of their long swords slapping against their legs. Their eyes were focused straight ahead. They ignored me completely since I was dressed as a peasant who could not possibly help them.

By the time they reached the farthest fish pond, I was already walking the provincial road on my return trip to Manila.

Unto this day, I do not know the names of the two Americans. To reveal their names would have been the death sentence to the one mentioning it. And if you heard it and were captured and tortured, you, in turn, might also reveal it.

However, it was rumored much later that one of them was Colonel Ramsey, leader of Ramsey's Guerrillas.

After several hours underwater, the two Americans were brought back to the surface.

When the sun began to set, their complexion would not be so apparent. It was impossible to hide white-faced Americans for very long in the open.

Later, a guide was assigned to bring them to another hiding place further into the interior of the jungle.

Unfortunately, several months later, I was an unwilling witness to a nerve-shattering confrontation with an American guerrilla colonel.

After conferring with Col. Barilea at his Balintawak hideout, five of us walked to Col. Dorsey's* jungle lair in Central Luzon.

With Captain Mohammed, a fierce-looking Moro at his side, a hot-headed Barilea announced he was an equal in rank and threatened to shoot the American on the spot unless he and his men became more aggressive. Barilea accused Dorsey of hiding in the jungle, thus jeopardizing other guerrilla cadres.

After a heated discussion, Col. Dorsey promised to be more active immediately.

Barilea and his men removed their hands from their weapons. He refused to shake hands with Dorsey.

When Barilea commanded us, *"Tayo-na"* or *"That's it! Let's go!"* we five guerrillas returned to our Balintawak headquarters.

Why Col. Barilea included me in his select group, I do not know. And I never had the courage to ask.

After his execution by Japanese, US Army Major C.A. Thorp's ID card was used as a "code password" by guerrillas.

---

* Name changed to protect identity.

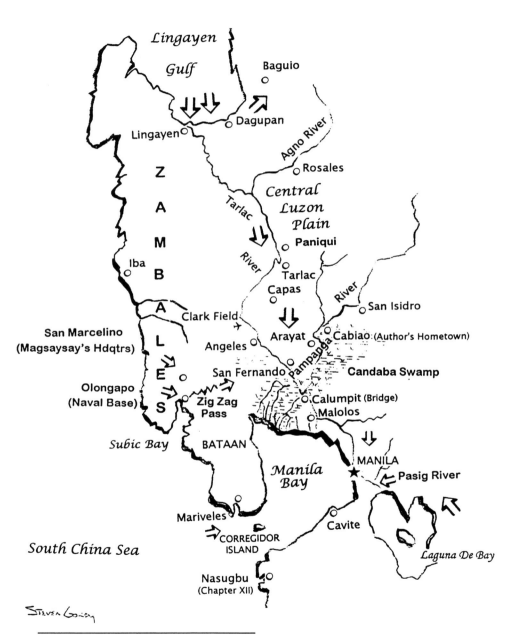

**American Return to Luzon
Philippine Islands**
(January 9, 1945)

Chapter 17

FROM LINGAYEN GULF TO MANILA

Very early in the morning of October 2, 1944, Commander Barilea summoned all members of the intelligence unit to his jungle hideout. He briefed us regarding the imminent arrival of General MacArthur's liberation forces on the island of Leyte in the Visayas, a group of islands in central Philippines.

Consequently, he ordered those under his command to leave the City of Manila immediately. "You all know that the enemy will make its last stand in Manila and in the Intramuros, (the walled city)" he commented. "We are certain that the thousands of soldiers plus Admiral Sanji Iwabuchi's 17,000 Navy men will surround the area," he snarled. "They will kill, burn and massacre whomever they find in the city when they are ordered to do so! Let's not fool ourselves! We have seen with our own eyes what they have done to us during the past three years of Occupation. Remember what happened in Nanking, China!"

He warned us to be stealthy and secretive but yet spread the news around the city. Then we who were non-combatants should travel north as fast as we could to await the landing of the American Liberation Forces somewhere in the Lingayen Gulf area.

I returned to my home place, gathered the family together and began the journey the only way we could afford—on foot! It was at least eighty miles to Tarlac Province. It took eight days! We were compelled to halt each day at dusk. People along the road were very kind to us, and a few invited us to stay in their homes for the night. They shared with us some of the little food that they had—even though we were strangers. We cannot remember their names, but they saved our lives. Once in a great while, we were fortunate enough to hitchhike a ride in an open market truck with no sidings or in an occasional dilapidated farm vehicle.

On the eighth day we stumbled into Anao, Tarlac, and went into seclusion on the farm of my in-laws. They advised us to leave the children and others with them for safekeeping when it was time for me to report for duty at Lingayen Gulf, around New Year's Day.

Oh! What a joy to feel secure and at rest with my beloved in-laws! After an existence of only one meal a day in Manila, when I could earn it, we were almost in luxury. Our daily Manila meal, when we could get it, consisted of a *chupa,* or cup, of rice, two or three small sweet potatoes and, occasionally, a coconut—for seven people! When I could not get work—we *did not* eat that day!

Our life in Manila had been desperate: the most difficult time of my daily existence was the nightly walking up the steps of our hideaway home in the Manila suburbs of San Juan with provisions—for only one meal.

Eduarda, one of my nannies, quickly opened and closed the apartment door without compromising the "black-out" status.

What a joyful contrast to be surrounded by my children and their nannies, Eduarda and Leona. Their rapid fire questions: "Mama, *gutum-na ako* (I'm sooooo hungry!) Are you all right? Where have you been? We missed you so much! I'm hungry! Please don't go away again! I'm hungry!" were interspersed with a multitude of kisses and hugs that would not let go.

Leona tended the small fire of sticks. Eduarda unfolded my bundled newspaper bag, poured out the *chupa* (handful) of rice and mixed it with a quart of water. When boiled it would expand sufficiently to fill seven hungry stomachs.

Occasionally we also were able to boil a tablespoon of tiny green "mung" beans (again with lots of water) for our protein.

We always had several small chunks of white coconut meat

covered with its brown hairy peel. After roasting them in the hot ashes, Eduarda smashed them with a hammer so that we all would have several mouthfuls.

While the meal was cooking, I bathed and washed my clothes with homemade lye soap in preparation for the next day's work.

Then came the children's recital of their daily activities inside the apartment. To avoid contact with the enemy, only Eduarda was permitted to go outside to gather broken tree limbs for our cooking fire. They showed me the pictures they had drawn, recalled the games they had played, the magazines read, noting the advertisements of Magnolia ice cream and especially the pictures of green beans and peas of Bird's Eye food—visions of a child's paradise of unobtainable delights.

The children quickly fell asleep after their only meal of the day.

Because of my imprisonment and 7-mile walk to Manila, my legs continued to swell and be painful.

I was unable to sleep until Eduarda and Leona had massaged my legs from the knee to the toes for at least 30 minutes.

Every morning we scraped the rice stains from the pot and boiled them along with any floating mosquitos. We then drank a cup for our breakfast.

Hugs! Kisses! and the 7-mile walk to Quiapo market to earn enough to keep us alive for another 24 hours. As I trudged along, I speculated, "When? Oh when will the Americans return to help us?

"How much longer can I personally endure my leg pains?

"If I die, I well know that the remnants of my family will all die of starvation like the dozens of bodies I see every morning in *Quiapo* and Far Eastern University areas.

"If I were sick: there is no money for medicine—and—no medicine.

"Oh, my God! Please help me buy and sell enough clothing and trinkets to have sufficient food for tonight's meal!"

Now we were on the farm where we could eat three times a day with simple but nourishing food. All we could do was thank the Lord for His loving care upon us.

A great surprise came on October 21st. As we were finishing breakfast, a stranger came to the front door with startling information.

"I am Major Severino Reyes," he revealed, "from the Pampanga Guerrillas under Colonel Mario Pamintuan. Colonel Barilea requested that I pass on some great news to you all. General MacArthur has just landed in Leyte!"

It was too good to be true! But he had some foolproof evidence. From deep inside his jacket and bedroll, he produced several fresh, unopened packs of Chesterfield cigarettes and a few bars of United States-manufactured GI snack peanut brittle. (He knew, of course, if he had been caught with these supplies, he would have been tortured and executed.)

That was all the proof we needed! When we saw those items, especially the American cigarettes, we knew that it was the absolute truth. The only way they could have arrived was *via* a submarine that had landed at Luzon. Obviously, these items, plus men, supplies and weapons had also been delivered along with our "goodies."

We were still living on the high of this experience, when in November we received an alert by another messenger, Captain Virgilio Evangelista. He ordered us to make preparations to depart town and go as far away as possible into the hills. The Japanese Army would be retreating south toward Manila in our direction when the U.S. Armed Forces landed in Lingayen Gulf.

By December 12, 1944, Anao, Paniqui and Moncada became ghost towns one more time. Nobody wanted to be around when the Japanese would come in strength. We had suffered too much already. Thus, the people were forced to hide again from the probable paths of a retreating and angry defeated army.

Our family enjoyed the Christmas season without presents, trees, balloons, lights, or any other decorations of a normal celebration. But we rejoiced, praying and thanking God, that very soon the American Armed Forces would be coming to liberate us from our three years of enemy occupation. Several cousins shared the results of their hunting expedition in a local *hacienda*. Using sharpened sticks, they had impaled dusky green frogs in an abandoned rice paddy. We each devoured two large frog thighs fried in coconut oil. How blessed was that Christmas!

On New Year's Day of 1945, I received an order from Colonel Barilea to proceed with caution from Tarlac Province to Lingayen. I would be accompanied by Rosa Aguire and Captain Villareal to anticipate the landing of the Americans.

He advised us to make certain our credentials were in order and that we should be ready to display our primitive "dog tags," to the Americans for instant identification.

So, once again, I tearfully parted from my children, but I knew that they would be well cared for by Dr. Jesus Evangelista and his family.

Upon arrival, we guerrilleros mixed with the civilian population in the Lingayen Area. How surprised we were one morning when we heard cannonading originating in the Gulf of Lingayen! January 9th, 1945 was D-Day!

Although we remained in jungle hideouts, we could observe the large warships anchored offshore and lobbing high-velocity shells into the jungles and beachheads. Soon, we saw hundreds of landing craft departing the mother ships and heading our way. Since the war had bypassed us, we did not know the names of all the vessels that were present. Later, it was explained to us that they were LSTs, LCIs, LSMs, LCVPs and others. We watched as they opened their bow doors, and tanks, jeeps and hundreds and hundreds of soldiers advanced toward the beaches.

After years of hearing technical words on our underground radios, we were now seeing these fantastic boats with our own eyes. Miraculous! Yet true!

As soon as we saw such a landing force of hundreds of vessels being unleashed, we knew that with time the Army would retake Manila and the entire Philippines. When the shelling stopped, the soldiers approached the tree line. At top speed, we ran out of the jungle and shouted for joy. Emerging from the low area of the bushes, many of us were screaming *"Mabuhay! Mabuhay!"* or "Hurrah! Victory!"

Imagine! Among the first group of soldiers was a contingent of Filipino-Americans! They were part of the First Filipino Division of the U.S. Army. It seemed like a master psychological stroke that we should meet some of our own countrymen so soon!

Unfortunately, several American warships were damaged or sunk by the Japanese Air Force. There were also human casualties sprawled on the beach.

After identifying myself, I returned with the invasion forces as they spearheaded south. Soon thereafter, I commandeered a horse and using a blanket as a saddle, I galloped toward the capital of Tarlac. I was directed to cross the Agno River and join the first PCAU (Philippine Civilian Affairs Unit 4) commanded by Major John Carlisle, of Carlisle, Pennsylvania. I became the first member of Barrion's Division to be attached officially to PCAU No. 4.

My initial mission was to scout around the far side of the Agno River for civilian refugee camps and for those who had been hiding from the Japanese army.

Less than five miles away, we discovered more than five hundred old men, women and children. There was practically no food and all were extremely hungry, sick and discouraged by having to sleep in the open fields.

Major Carlisle immediately ordered the soldiers to give the victims some bread and other available food and blankets. The PCAU-4 remained more than a week as we assisted those folks and strengthened them for their next task. As part of the rehabilitation process, they were advised to return to their homes as soon as they were liberated from enemy domination, as the Japanese retreated to the Sierra Madre and Cordillera mountains.

Crossing a more distant bend in the river, the PCAU soldiers encountered another group of refugees with many, many children who had fled from the rampaging, retreating Japanese Army.

My daughter Betty with other members of the extended family remembered it well. As a preteenager, she likened it to the atmosphere of a summer camp. After securing the area, the Army set up a small city of tents for the refugees and brought in bundles of food including fresh-baked loaves of white bread. They had neither seen nor eaten American food for more than three years. Even emergency "C" and "K" rations seemed like ambrosia to them. Large bonfires were built by the soldiers, and as they finished their supper, everybody gathered around to share.

The soldiers taught them the latest popular U.S. songs such as "Paper Doll" and "God Bless America."

Then they all joined together in singing the old favorites that were familiar to everybody: "Home On The Range," "My Old Kentucky Home," and "Jeannie With The Light Brown Hair." Jeep driver, Sergeant William Brown, and Johnnie Stryker of Chicago were especially memorable singers, as they were accompanied by a virtuoso Filipino guitarist from Pampanga Province. Finally, near midnight, the soldiers had to return to their campsite as we all joined in a rousing farewell with "The Star Spangled Banner." Everybody shouted "Victory Joe!" and *Mabuhay!"* No Filipino ever forgot that night of victory and happiness with their newly found American friends—even after 50 years!

As the liberation forces marched toward Manila, PCAU-4 and soon PCAU-5 followed them very closely. At Balintawak, a few miles north of Manila, my unit bivouacked about one mile from the artillery division. As we went about our refugee rehabilitation during the next few days, we could hardly hear each other because of the deafening bombardment of Manila. There was no real forward progress at this point, only that the infantry went out and then returned.

At last the Army broke through to the next destination in Manila, with Bilibid Prison as the objective. On January 24, 1945, PCAU-4 was ordered to go in on the northwest side of Manila and reach the prison. Theoretically, the path had been cleared and was free of enemy snipers. Word reached us that all bridges had been demolished by the Japanese as they retreated. We observed that Santo Tomas University Internment Camp had been liberated and its 4,000 Americans and other Allied prisoners were now free and could receive food and medicine. We cheered them on with *"Mabuhay!"*

Manila is divided by the Pasig River. The destruction of all the

bridges made it that much more difficult for the advancing liberation forces. It was part of the Japanese strategy. While debating
what to do next, we saw two squads of American soldiers taking a
coffee break. They passed on the news that a pontoon bridge had
just been completed from Nagtahan Road to Sampaloc to the Paco
District. It was now safe to proceed.

Unfortunately, the Paco district had been reduced to rubble
and ashes. Thousands of residents had been burned alive because

The Destruction of Manila
(February, 1945)

the retreating Japanese troops and *Makapilis* (or traitors), had poured kerosene and torched innumerable homes and buildings throughout the subdivisions of Ermita, Malate and Paco. Those who were not incinerated by the maddened Japanese had been massacred. More than 100,000 charred and mutilated bodies littered the desolate area.

Léon, my adventurous jeep driver-bodyguard, disobeyed orders and determined to see for himself the massacre in Ermita. We passed street after street where every house had been bombed and burned into absolute destruction. We saw countless remnants of one or two concrete steps that led to the empty sky. Other sites had three battered steps facing a hole the approximate size of a home. Then there would be an expanse of 50 to 60 feet of fist-sized chunks of concrete—of what were formerly concrete-built houses. If the houses had been constructed of wood, there would only be a blackened area of ash. Nothing was higher than three to four inches. The wind blew the stench of burned bodies and kerosene throughout the area.

Legislature Building

Another 100 yards further north on the street, we heard the *rat-a-tat-tat* of Japanese machine guns. Civilians were running in all directions. We watched in horror as many of them screamed in pain and fell to the ground and moved no more.

American soldiers intervened and silenced the machine guns.

We followed a squad of soldiers who were aiding the victims. We assisted a few of the fear-stricken survivors, including Senator Elpidio Quirino and his young daughter, Vicky. His wife had been killed as she was running from the Japanese troops. Later, Mr. Quirino became President of the Philippines.

Shaking with fright, Léon turned the jeep around, picked up a few trembling survivors and retreated at top speed to where we were supposed to be—PCAU-4, assisting another group of refugees in our allotted area. He never acted so foolhardy or was disobedient again.

I recalled Colonel Barilea's explicit warning several months before, predicting this exact scenario.

A passing Filipino-American with tears in his eyes, described

President's Office—Malacanan

to us that thousands of civilians were still trapped in the Intramuros, the glamorous walled city built by the Spaniards three centuries before. Indeed, several months after the battle was over, I met one of my dearest friends, Cristeta Angeles, who told me that her husband, retired Major D. Angeles, former Military Governor of the Sulu Archipelago, and her two teenage sons had been trapped and massacred in the Intramuros. They were but three of thousands who had been butchered by the well-entrenched Japanese Army.

The Intramuros was the center of the final Japanese resistance. Its stone walls were 25 feet high and 40 feet thick, making a formidable defense system!

The Japanese rejected several American offers of honorable surrender. The only recourse was to subject the fortress to endless bombing and artillery fire. The American troops fought painfully and dangerously, building by building, room by room and foot by foot with machine guns, hand grenades and finally, flame throwers. The enemy was hidden behind every crevice and corner and

Wrecked Building—Escolta Street
(elite shopping district)

lurked inside basements and storage cells in both public buildings and churches. The magnificent Manila Cathedral and all other churches were obliterated with the exception of San Augustine Church.

Even the secluded Carmelite nuns, as they prayed, were bayoneted and left to die in puddles of blood on the floor of the chapel.

Searching for still more survivor-refugees in Azcarraga Street, we came under the guardian wing of several squads of American soldiers. They were attempting to "clean out" a pocket of enemy soldiers hidden inside a classroom building of Far Eastern University.

With bullets zinging around us, the Americans finally crossed the street and liberated the inhabitants of the building.

They then signaled us to join them. The street was so littered with dead bodies of Japanese soldiers that we were compelled to walk across their soft flesh.

Behind the protective cover of a wall, the sergeant announced it was 1:00 P.M. and time to take a lunch break. The GIs sat down on the chests and across the backs of the still warm corpses of the recently killed enemy soldiers. I dared not stand up and be an inviting target for a sniper, so I also had to sit on the bodies.

They shared their lunch rations with us, but I decided to decline the offer of food under those bloody and grisly circumstances.

An almost identical scenario occurred a month later when I served as a Special Correspondent for *YANK, The Army Weekly* at San Pablo, Laguna. During my interviews with the American soldiers a short distance from the front-line action, we were again informed it was lunchtime. Everybody plumped down amidst the hundreds of dead enemy troops. My companion, Nati Borja, ate both her sandwiches as well as mine. I just sipped a canteen cup of coffee and continued with the interviews. My appetite was gone again.

After lunch, we followed the GIs around the University walls and reached the initial group of refugees. We PCAU-ers went to work assisting them, even as the Americans went about their soldier work at the next intersection.

Finally, on March 3rd, the last pockets of resistance in the Finance Building were silenced. The City of Manila was now secure except for occasional nighttime sniper firing.

The only major battle for a city in the War in the Pacific had cost the lives of over 100,000 civilian Filipinos. In Europe, only Warsaw suffered a greater destruction than Manila.

A wretched aftermath of the genocidal breakdown was the sight of hundreds of orphaned children wandering aimlessly about the ruins screaming, "Mama! Mama! Where are you?" Others just sat forlornly on debris and stared into space.

I could not do everything, but I determined to do something to alleviate a part of the suffering.

Aided by my journalist friend, Esther Lerma, we persuaded a sympathetic widow in the suburb of San Juan to open her three-story house to these waifs.

I was able to transfer 27 children, ages nine to fourteen, to the home and arrange for twelve clubwomen to provide them with food on a daily basis and to maintain a haven for them until further notice.

Members of US Army Guerrilla Recognition Team (center), Mrs. Antiporda, Mrs. Block, Major Faustino Antiporda, with leaders of Antiporda Regiment—1948 (See Chapter 15—Missing in Action—In Cement)

Chapter 18

U.S.O.—PHILIPPINE STYLE

After more than a month's service with PCAU-4, Colonel Barilea recalled me to the HQ Unit of Barrion's Division. Now, I was dispatched to San Francisco del Monte, a suburb of Manila. Although Manila was comparatively peaceful, our instructions were to be extremely cautious. We were stationed adjacent to the Army outfits that kept bombarding the enemy concentrations at nearby Marikina.

Not long after, Colonel Barilea suggested, actually ordered, that I organize a Division Committee to plan a party of thanksgiving for the General Headquarters of General MacArthur.

"Lt. Blanco," he stated, "you will have a fiesta, or party, of Philippine culinary delights for them. We want the men to procure and serve barbecued *lechon* (whole roast baby pig), plus chicken *adobo*. The ladies will prepare homemade specialties—*pancit* (rice noodles), *lumpia* (tiny, delicate egg rolls), etc.

"When you are ready, call the Executive Officer, Captain Shubert of U.S. Army HQ and invite all the staff."

The following day Captain Shubert saw to it that everybody came out *en masse* including General Charles Willoughby, General Courtney Whitney and Hollywood celebrities such as Lanny Ross, Lew Ayres, and Earl Carroll.

We made sure nobody would ever have any problem finding our cantina at Barrion's Headquarters. His division adjutant had stationed two men at quarter-mile intervals from Manila to our HQ. Each man carried a large placard with a shiny arrow pointing in the right direction.

The party was a huge success. As a result, Lanny Ross, then a Special Service Officer with GHQ, suggested to Colonel Barilea that I should initiate a makeshift USO until the war settled down. That would then give the Army sufficient time to bring the regular USO from Hollandia, New Guinea, to Manila.

Subsequently, Colonel Barilea also appointed me as Chairman of Entertainment for groups of Army, Navy and Air Force officers.

My friends, the Borja family, who had sustained me so much during the Occupation, again came to the rescue.

They offered their beautiful home for the parties since our HQ was too distant from the center of the city.

Mr. Borja was a member of the Manila law firm of Dewitt, Perkins, & Ponce Enrile. His son, Horacio, was a university professor of violin; Nati, his daughter, was my classmate in a Manila "Finishing School"—La Consolacion College. She later became Professor of Piano at the University of the Philippines.

Another unsung heroine of the war was Mrs. Borja. On numerous occasions, she hid and fed various guerrilla leaders during the Occupation. One slip of the tongue, one glance from a *Makapili* and they would have all perished. Their house also would have been confiscated or burned to the ground.

Now, they were only too happy to open their residence again to their American friends and liberators. Dinner was usually served at 7:00 P.M., followed by a program of singing and sharing by volunteers who spoke for five minutes each about what was in their hearts. Adjournment was at 10:00 P.M.

Captain Shubert of New York gave me some strange advice regarding how to plan. He believed that it was for the betterment of all concerned if only one group of service officers were invited on any one evening. For example: Monday—Army; Tuesday—Navy; Wednesday—Air Force, etc. "Never mix outfits," he cautioned. "It makes for better relationships among the Armed Forces."

Many Manila socialites generously gave of their time and energies to help run the canteen. They arrived with whatever type of refreshments that they were able to locate in the local markets.

Their conversation and musical presentations were a plus. It was a welcome relief for those Americans fighting on the front lines just to the south of the city. What a pleasure to relax in a home environment for even a short period of time before they went back to the business of war.

When asked as to which were the most interesting, the Army, Navy, or the Army Air Force, the volunteers all agreed diplomatically that "they were all wonderful gentlemen, brave, but mostly homesick." They also concurred, "It was such a little gesture of appreciation we could show them for their helping free us from our enemies." (Whether it was from loneliness or love, I received marriage proposals from two majors and one captain!)

Lanny Ross of Hollywood usually led the singing at these interservice parties. It was a delight to hear all those male voices! Some reawakened their talents for music and sang solo to the pleasure and jokes of the others. Everyone's special song was "You Are My Sunshine." It almost became the National Anthem of the Philippines. Other favorites were "Don't Sit Under The Apple Tree With Anyone Else But Me" and "Paper Doll."

Lew Ayres was "something else" in those days, since he could keep a straight face while relating a dry-humored story. Meanwhile, everybody else would be laughing until their faces turned a deep red.

The Naval officers were commendable in their selection of refreshments. They always brought difficult-to-obtain items such as genuine coffee, white sugar and canned cream. However, their overcooked oatmeal cookies were tough and chewy. I silently wished that there would be no broken teeth since we didn't have any dental officers among the guests.

The majority of the officers preferred the native Filipino *Bibingka* (rice cake). It was made of sticky rice cooked in coconut milk with sugar on top. *Flan*, a rich Spanish custard consisting of egg yolks and milk topped with caramel sauce, disappeared very quickly.

Mrs. Borja, always a perfect hostess, usually prepared the main course of pork and chicken *adobo*. *Pancit* (thin rice noodles) with stir-fried shrimp was voraciously eaten.

One evening, when Mrs. Borja had cooked these delicacies and placed them on the serving table, a major from Indiana surprised us by *somersaulting* all the way from the living room to the dinner table to show his appreciation. He loved these Filipino dishes, having tasted them before.

Whenever he came, he always led the procession to the serving tables by somersaulting from the living room to the platters heaped with food.

Chapter 19

CAPTAIN TO COLONEL IN FIVE MINUTES

Commander Barilea hurriedly summoned me to report to his headquarters outside Manila on April 15, 1945. Upon my arrival, he assigned me to special duty to the General Headquarters of the U.S. Army in Manila. He asserted, "Be prepared to meet two Army officers who are attached to a recognition team that is investigating several guerrilla divisions claiming official recognition from the U.S. Army."

Barilea said, "You are knowledgeable about the Magsaysay guerrillas of Zambales and the Pamintuan regiment of Pampanga. I am sure you can help tremendously to verify these and other outfits since you have been delivering secret messages to them during the resistance years. I feel confident you can aid them on their fact-finding mission."

I immediately accepted.

Arriving at the Army GHQ office, I was quickly presented to Captain George Shubert who in turn introduced Colonel Pachtel and another officer.

After checking and verifying my credentials, Captain Shubert inquired, "Do you have your driver's license?"

I pulled my tattered, but still-valid Manila driver's license from my wallet.

"Okay!" he advised. "Here is your trip ticket. Present it to the Base Motor Pool Officer downstairs who will assign you a jeep.

Drive down to Zambales Province immediately and find Captain Magsaysay. These other gentlemen will meet you there tomorrow."

This would be a choice assignment, because I had recently been hired as a special reporter by the editor, Vicente Del Fierro, for the Manila daily newspaper, *The Star Reporter*. Del Fierro was doing a series of articles on guerrilla recognition. He was fully aware that there were many opportunistic people who did not serve honorably during the war and yet claimed to be true allies of the United States.

I still remember his exasperation as he shouted, "If there were really that many guerrillas during the Occupation we could have driven the Japanese out of our country, or killed them—man to man!"

As I circled around the hairpin curves of Zig Zag Pass in Zambales, I could still see the destruction of war on both sides of the road. The U.S. Army had recently liberated it. The only danger now was from an occasional sniper.

The Magsaysay Headquarters was located in the town of San Marcelino, not too far from the Subic Naval Base.

After greeting Captain Magsaysay, the first thing that claimed my attention was the insignia on his collar lapels. He had the two silver bars of a Captain!

Yet, he claimed to be the Commander of a full division of men. I made a reportorial mental note: "How can he be only a captain when he is a division commander? When we get to a PX, we'll fix that up!"

Knowing that I was a journalist, Magsaysay naturally wanted to share everything that he could regarding his outfit. As he displayed all his pertinent records that had survived, he constantly paced back and forth and cracked first the knuckles of his left hand, and then those of his right.

Starting with only a handful of trusted friends, but imbued with patriotic fervor for the United States, he was able to persuade hundreds of his fellow provincemates of Zambales to join in the Resistance with him. In a little under a year, he had recruited an entire regiment.

Later, he graciously invited me to lunch and to meet his wife and family. Mrs. Magsaysay seemed to be a very modest lady, sweet and remarkably self-effacing.

Next I traveled to the nearby town of San Antonio to verify several of his accounts. Miss Apostol, a local teacher, was my hostess and one of the knowledgeable informants.

I returned the following day to the Magsaysay headquarters and was present as the two-man team of the Army Officer Recognition Unit grilled him for further information. While listening to Magsaysay, I observed how humbly and unpretentiously he talked about his men and his division. I was convinced that he had truly served the cause of the nation's fight for freedom.

Also, I found he was an impatient and restless man. He was worried and wondered how the team would act on the recognition of his men. "They were very loyal and sacrificed so much during the past three years. Some died in the line of duty. I hope they will act soon. What do you think they will do?" he inquired. Again he stretched his fingers backward until I heard popping sounds.

In response, I countered, "I suggest that you and your wife take all your essential papers and return with me to Manila. I'll bring you to the U.S. Army GHQ for Guerrilla Affairs. Then you can consult with the 'higher-ups' and you'll probably have much better results."

He slapped his hands together vigorously, "I agree! When you return here tomorrow from Miss Apostol's home, we'll journey together."

Shortly after breakfast the next day, we went to San Marcelino to pick up the Magsaysays in my GHQ jeep. On the road to Zig Zag Pass, I suggested that we stop by the U.S. Navy Base in Olongapo and buy an appropriate insignia for him at the Officers' PX.

"You will what?" he laughed. "You'll buy me a pin?" he asked as he shrugged his shoulders.

"Well," I explained, "if you have a full division of men, as you said, then you have to be at least a Colonel in rank. My leader, Colonel Barilea, rightfully wears them. Don't you think that is the best way?"

Within the hour, at the Navy PX, I personally bought the silver eagle insignia of a colonel. Then, his wife and I pulled him toward a corner and made him stand still. I whispered, "Luz, *alisin mo ang insigniya*" or "Take off the captain's bars!" I quickly pinned the proper insignia on his collar, as befitting the commander of a division. He was all smiles. Then we all shook hands with the new colonel and congratulated him. Again, he cracked his knuckles.

Officially, he was now Colonel Ramon Magsaysay, Leader of the Magsaysay Guerrillas of Zambales!

If there were any snipers or stragglers in Zig Zag Pass, they must have all been hiding as we slowly negotiated the steep mountainous curves in a torrential downpour. Many hours later we arrived safely in Manila. In order to dry their rain-soaked clothing and make them look more presentable, I escorted them to the Borja home where they could refresh themselves. The Borja family received them as friends and set forth a hearty *merienda* and hot coffee at about 3:00 P.M.

Then it was time to visit the Army GHQ. I introduced them to the Intelligence Officer, General Charles Willoughby.

The rest is history!

Little did I comprehend on that day that this same man would later become a Congressman and eventually be elected as the President of the Philippines.

As we were preparing to depart, Captain Shubert informed Colonel Magsaysay that I was the lady who had organized and formed a committee for entertaining war-weary officers as they rested a few days before going back into action on the south front lines. I overheard, "Look into it!"

Perhaps that planted a seed in Magsaysay's mind to do the same in his own province. Accordingly, he invited me to return to Zambales and help organize the ladies there to initiate a similar type USO Club for the liberating forces of the Army, Navy and Army Air Force.

After Magsaysay consulted with my boss, Colonel Barilea, they concluded it was a superb idea and that it should start immediately.

Using Miss Apostol's home in San Antonio as a base, we organized the female school teachers, doctors, nurses and others to initiate parties, dinner-dances, etc., to be held at the Municipal Building or City Hall in that town. Later, we expanded to San Marcelino and San Narcisco, as well. It soon became a highlight time for those who so much needed recreation and release from the agonies of the front-line fighting.

However, I never again saw an officer somersaulting to the tables laden with food.

I felt it a special calling and pleasure to help in such a manner. But, once it was functioning well, I knew it was time for me to return to Manila and help my own division alongside Colonel Barilea.

Army Trip Ticket for GHQ Jeep
(stolen from Jeep at US Naval Base)

Chapter 20

A FLY IN THE OINTMENT

On the way home from San Antonio, I decided to take a coffee break at the Naval Base at Olongapo, Subic Bay. It would be a "pep-up stop" to help me keep awake and alert as I manuevered my way through Zig Zag Pass. I noticed every Naval officer was staring at me as I parked my jeep a few feet from the door to the Officers' PX tent.

What could be the problem? Was it perhaps the first time that a jeep marked GHQ, Intelligence Division had been seen in Zambales? It marked me as being closely linked to General MacArthur's Headquarters in Manila, and the Navy wanted no part of its nemesis on their turf.

I brought my coffee cup to a table. For the first time in three years, I saw in a small container—actual refined *white* sugar. It was a touch of heaven to be able to place a spoonful of white sugar in my coffee and enjoy it. Surprisingly, when I reached for the sugar bowl, several officers laughed openly at me. I ignored them and enjoyed the American coffee and white sugar.

On the way out, a stocky Lieutenant, Senior Grade scowled at me and looked derisively at the sugar bowl. He came close to me and growled, "Where did *you*—get that jeep? Did you *steal* it?"

I ignored his comment, but as I went to the jeep glove compartment to show him my GHQ trip ticket, I noticed that it was no longer in place!

Noticing my chagrin and half-empty glove compartment, he mocked, "You cannot drive this jeep. You stole it from the Army. I am placing you under arrest!"

Keeping my cool, I ignored his statement, took my seat and drove off.

However, at the main checkout gate, an armed shore-patrol guard pointed his automatic rifle at me. He ordered, "Get out! Stick your hands in the air!"

Naturally, I complied.

He barked, "Lt. Senior Grade Freer ordered me to confiscate this jeep from you!" As I was standing alone on the dusty road, I suddenly realized that the man who had scowled at me in the Officers' Club was the same officer.

Looking at his badge of authority, I was too shocked to understand anything that was happening. I internalized, "Could it be that because I am a woman, a Filipina . . . that I don't fit in their picture of what I should be? Perhaps Lt. Freer thought it impossible that an Army woman guerrilla, "a nobody," could ever be given a GHQ jeep! Or, could it be that an Army person was not welcomed or allowed in a Naval facility?"

I recalled how often I had been told while establishing our Filipino USOs that we would not be able to give a party at the Borja residence if we mixed officers from the different services. But, what was the right answer for my mind that was so confused by this sudden turn of events?

After a short conference at gunpoint, I was ordered back to Manila. A driver-guide officer was my escort.

Upon arrival, I was not taken to AFWESPAC (Armed Forces of Western Pacific) HQ.

Instead, they escorted me to Muntinglupa Prison!

Chapter 21

WHY AM I IN PRISON?

The officer guard physically delivered me to the Officer-in-Charge of the Muntinglupa Prison. Captain Tweedle, U.S. Army, was a tall, very friendly woman from Harrisburg, Pennsylvania. After taking me to the Mess Hall, if you could call it that, I drank a cup of bitter coffee and asked her, "What is this place? Why am I here?"

Her answer staggered me. "This is a Women's Prison for all the collaborators and traitors that have been rounded up so far by the Army. They will be incarcerated here until further investigation is made regarding their activities. And you—are our prisoner!"

Immediately, I exclaimed, "Why is it that you did not have papers for me? If I am a prisoner, why didn't you process my papers?"

Captain Tweedle stated, "Tomorrow morning, Colonel Hall of AFWESPAC (Armed Forces of Western Pacific) will come to brief you." As she muttered these words, she tilted her head upward while looking downward at me with disdain in her eyes. She motioned for an armed guard to follow us.

"Meantime," she mumbled, "follow me!" She brusquely led me to the first floor of a brick-lined musty large hall that had been hurriedly converted into a dormitory. Army cots arranged side by side, six to each aisle, were jammed against the wall of the room.

Each bed was marked with the name of its occupant. The first three were Attorney Clara La Paz,* Mrs. Soo R. Tien* and Ana Mirable.* They and the others were all well-known names. The

---

* Names have been changed to protect identity of "Manila's 400."

twelfth cot had my name on it.

Surprised, dazed, humiliated, I was careful not to say anything to antagonize the captain.

The next morning, after what passed for a prison breakfast, I found Captain Tweedle in the hallway and confronted her again about my mysterious situation.

"Answer me! Why was I brought to this prison without due process? Without any legal papers? Am I supposed to be a collaborator? How can you do this to me—a guerrilla intelligence officer?"

She refused to answer. She looked the other way and again summoned a sentry to escort me back to the dormitory.

Leaving the dining hall one afternoon, Miss de la Cruz,* a prominent young socialite, astounded me with the revelation that she was the one directly responsible for my prior imprisonment (and torture) at Ft. Santiago. She tittered, "You know, it was nothing personal. Just something that had to be done in those days."

"And now—just look," she laughed nervously, "we're all in the same boat together—prisoners in Muntinglupa Prison!"

"Hee! Hee! Hee!" she giggled, "don't worry, I'll be on top again in a very short time. I'll invite you to my next party."

All her friends echoed her giggling.

After seven days with no explanation whatsoever, Captain Tweedle finally began to process me as a legitimate prisoner. Meantime, nobody was aware of my plight. I had completely dropped out of sight as if I had been missing in action.

I requested her to telephone Captain Shubert at GHQ since he was the one who authorized me to use that now-infamous GHQ-Intelligence jeep. I had presumed that it was the center of all this controversy. Around noon, having made me wait for several hours, she finally announced that a Colonel Hall was waiting to see me.

"Surprise! Surprise!" Colonel Hall greeted me. "I just checked with Captain George Shubert. He confirmed your authorization regarding a trip ticket for a GHQ jeep that you used in your investigation of the guerrillas. It was legitimately assigned to you as

---

* Name changed to protect identity.

part of the Investigation Team of the Guerrilla Affairs Division.

"It is unfortunate you were treated so harshly and undeservedly by the Olongapo naval officers," he continued.

"Guess what? Your stolen trip ticket was found in the purse of a woman who was occasionally with you—the one who claimed that she was a member of a rival guerrilla outfit." He personally thought it was a case of revenge or a political vendetta.

```
                                    31 August        1945

                              APO      75


SUBJECT:  Release of    BLANCO, Mamerta


TO      :  The Provost Marshal      Welfareville        APO   75


        1.  It is requested that Subject person or persons be
            released from confinement without delay.

        2.  Remarks:

            (a)  Subject was interned 11 July 1945 under
                 commitment order #732 charged with imper-
                 sonating a United States Army Intelligence
                 Officer.

            (b)  Subject is a Filipino Citizen.

            (c)  An investigation by this office did not re-
                 veal sufficient evidence to warrant further
                 internment.




                                    T.D. SMITH, Jr.
                                    Major, Cav.
                                    Commanding
```

Prison Release Authorization Form
(from unjustified imprisonment)

"Now, for the good news! You are *NO* longer a prisoner! You are free!"

There were *no* apologies.

He offered me a ride from the Muntinglupa Jail to Manila where I could be reunited with my friends at the Borja home in Quiapo.

Mrs. Borja was overwhelmed with joy to see me safe and alive. According to Filipino custom, she invited the Colonel to stay for coffee and refreshment as part of the afternoon *merienda* (snack).

Declining graciously, he apologized, "I am scheduled to fly to Hong Kong to meet my fiancee, Margaret Higgins, the war correspondent. We are going to be married."

Until this day, nobody, American or Filipino, has ever apologized to me!

As soon as Colonel Hall departed, Mrs. Borja cornered me and inquired, "It's been three weeks! What happened to you? You just disappeared and nobody knew where you were. Three weeks!"

Chapter 22

DISILLUSIONED

Seated quietly in their living room, I enumerated to them what had happened. It all began over a spoonful of white sugar in Olongapo Naval Base: my arrest by command of a senior officer, the trip to Muntinglupa and my ignominious imprisonment. Mr. Borja went to his desk and began to take notes.

Attorney Borja, a member of the well-known legal firm of Dewitt, Perkins, and Ponce Enrile, had risked not only his life but also those of his family. They had delivered food and medicine to the American members of his firm and others who were interned at Santo Tomas Concentration Camp for almost three years. They had also successfully hidden many guerrilla members in their home without arousing the suspicion of the Japanese who were only a few hundred yards away.

Mr. Borja's reaction after the recital of my woes was one of exasperation and disbelief. He hit the ceiling! Mrs. Borja arose and hugged me. She turned to her husband, "What will you do? Aren't you going to take legal action against those perpetrators of evil against Mamerta?"

Hiding his rage, he quietly went to his study. When he reappeared, about half an hour later, he requested me to read a legal document he had prepared: essentially, my "Complaint."

After signing it, he said, "I will see what I can do. But, first, we will try to contact Colonel Barilea and ascertain what he knows about all these misadventures." As he picked up his white Panama hat to depart to his office, the doorbell rang several times.

It was Colonel Barilea!

After we were all seated again in the living room, a very angry and indignant Attorney Borja demanded an immediate explanation from him regarding this atrocious conduct on the part of both the U.S. Navy and AFWESPAC (Armed Forces of Western Pacific).

Calmly, Colonel Barilea explained in detail what had occurred, according to what his agents had learned about my case.

"Mamerta was detached from Barrion's Division to the U.S. Special Guerrilla Verification Team," he began. "Next Captain Shubert assigned her a GHQ jeep to travel to Zambales to help verify the authenticity of Magsaysay's Guerrilla Outfit and another rival group. She was, at the same time, authorized by the Department of the Interior of the Philippines to travel wherever and whenever necessary to any place on Luzon Island on a fact-finding tour as investigative reporter for the *The Star Reporter*.

"It soon became obvious to some leaders of the guerrilla units that she would report the truth. Therefore, some pseudo-guerrilla groups tried to undermine her trip in order not to jeopardize their own false claims. They all wanted back-pay recognition money from the United States Army.

"They 'planted' a woman member to accompany Mamerta and be her guide in Zambales. Some members of the Magsaysay Guerrillas felt that Mamerta was going to report the truth that not all those on the roster were genuine active guerrillas. They ordered this woman to steal the trip ticket from the glove compartment of the jeep, where Captain George Shubert, Executive Officer of MacArthur's GHQ, had placed it for safekeeping.

"To further complicate matters, there was that surprise at the U.S. Navy Base in Olongapo. When they saw a petite Filipina, dressed as an officer, wearing a First Lieutenant's insignia and driving a GHQ Intelligence jeep from General MacArthur's Headquarters, that topped it off! It was too great an affront to their pride!

"Then Mamerta made another fatal 'faux pas.' She stopped at the Naval Officers' Mess Hall and attempted to buy a cup of coffee. She did the unthinkable: she asked for some of their precious white sugar as a sweetener!

"That—did it!

"To the Senior Lieutenant on duty, it was impossible to believe that a non-American and especially a brown-skinned Filipina could be an officer, much less be in possession of a GHQ Intelligence Division Army jeep. And how could she possibly request *white* sugar for her coffee—wasn't Filipino brown sugar good enough for her and her kind?"

Attorney Borja interrupted at this point: "I was just on my way to file a legal suit for Mamerta for this unseemly indignity poured out upon her by the U.S. Army and Navy. I have known Mamerta for almost all her life. She went with my daughter, Nati, to the same classes at La Consolacion College. They were like sisters growing up together. I have not seen a streak of meanness in her. She served our nation without reservation; for the entirety of the Japanese Occupation, she suffered indignities, tortures and imprisonment in Fort Santiago. And, in return, the Americans treated her like a despicable outcast and a criminal."

Colonel Barilea interrupted his outburst and then shocked us with this revelation:

"We are in the process of organizing the Philippine Veterans Legion and its Manila Chapter. During Mamerta's absence while touring Zambales, we Legionnaires elected her as Public Relations Officer of the Manila Chapter. She is an official member of Barrion's which, in turn, is duly recognized as a legitimate part of the U.S. Army. We need a fearless and just crusader like her to lead our veterans who are still fighting for the recognition rights of their service in World War II.

"The veterans planned to ask her to lead a mission to Washington, D.C. for the Philippine veterans, guerrillas, war widows and orphans. We believe she could do it with God's help and blessing. In the past, there were groups sent by our Government to the U.S.—our Senators, Congressmen and high-ranking Cabinet Members—to petition that the $100 million fund earmarked for payment of veterans with resistance service and later returned to the U.S. Treasury, be reactivated. But, they all have failed.

"We are hoping with Mamerta's faith in God and the power of

the Holy Spirit that she experienced during the resistance movement, that blessings will fall upon our suffering war widows and
orphans," he concluded.

Attorney Borja remained uncharacteristically silent. But, as
they parted for the evening, he remarked, "There's too much dis-
parity. We will see, we will see."

But, in my disgust and disillusionment, I shouted, "I have
done my part for three years. My family suffered much. My
brother and father were brutally massacred by the enemy; I lost
my husband, home and all my worldly possessions. I have done
and given enough. My family, my children all were secondary. My
country and America's cause came first. In return, there is this continued affront to my person. I am through, *kaput,* no more! *Hasta la
vista*, Colonel!"

However the following day, my cousin, Colonel Ismael Lapus,
Commander, Intelligence Division, Philippine Army HQ visited
me at the Borja home. He was accompanied by Attorney Jaime Fer-
rer, Major Faustino Antiporda of Rizal Province and General
Macario Peralta.

They all attempted to convince me to accept an active part in
the concentrated effort of fighting for the proper recognition of the
genuine active guerrillas and for the rights of the legitimate veterans. General Peralta was exceptionally persuasive. He and my deceased husband were longtime friends from the same hometown,
and as he made his appeal he almost persuaded me to re-enlist as
an active officer again.

I finally agreed to be the PRO (Public Relations Officer) and
radio spokesman for the guerrillas and to initiate a regularly
scheduled veterans program in the English language on KZPI
radio station.

Prior to this event, Vicente Del Fierro, the editor of the Manila
daily newspaper, *The Star Reporter*, employed me as a full-time active investigative reporter.

The years 1945-47 were a busy time of filing claims: veterans,
war damage, personal. But, I had a very interesting special claim
come into my own personal life in early 1945.

Chapter 23

FLAT TIRE LEADS TO LOVE

On my second trip to Zambales, driving out of the confines of the tortuous turns of Zig Zag Pass through the Zambales Mountains, I had a flat tire about a mile from the Navy Base Motor Pool. I slowly thumped my way into the Motor Pool where the Officer-in-Charge, Commander Chafee, looked, whistled and assigned a mechanic to fix my tire. In return, I offered him some of the delicious, tree-ripened Philippine mangos with smooth ice cream-like texture that I had on the back seat.

As the Commander invited me to rest a few minutes in his steamy canvas office tent, I noticed a thin ensign sitting in the far corner. His skin was stained yellow by the antimalarial drug Atrabine, and he appeared morose and bored. Greeting him cheerfully, I also offered him some of the mangos. He thanked me as he took the top one. But I had to show him how to peel it so it could be eaten. I was especially intrigued by his quiet demeanor. I think it was an example of love at first sight!

When the tire repair work was completed, I thanked them and said my goodbyes.

Several weeks later, when I returned to the area to organize the ladies of San Marcelino and San Antonio to inaugurate a USO-type party for the officers of the Army, Air Force and Navy, the same ensign came to the party for the naval officers. We found it very hard to dance, because he and many of the others were wearing combat boots.

Later, he invited me to the newly installed movies at the navy base. Of course, the only legitimate dating in the Philippines at that time included chaperones. This held back the natural processes, but it kept things on an informal basis.

One evening, during the movies we suddenly heard lots of automatic rifle fire behind us. We ducked, thinking it was a sneak enemy attack. But, we soon found out that all the gunfire was aimed at a 25-foot python in a treetop above the audience. Suddenly, the branches and the snake fell.

Everybody ran for safety! Nobody wanted to find out where it landed.

When the projectionist returned the next morning, only the broken tree branches were on the ground. All movies were canceled for one week.

Later, after a whirlwind courtship, we were married.

Motor Pool "Office" at NABU-6, Subic Bay, Philippines
(Ensign Isaac Block shown at lower right in both photos)

Chapter 24

THE BIG BEER SCANDAL

My weekly radio broadcast for the veterans on KZPI soon became a very popular program throughout the entire Philippines. High officials of the U.S. Veterans Administration, War Damage Claim Commission and others were interviewed regarding the acute problems of the Filipino veterans. Thousands of war widows sent in letters of inquiry and in desperation, through the station, sought help and guidance. Some were called in to share their problems with the audience.

I continued to work daily with *The Star Reporter*. A journalistic highlight took place as the Manila press began to probe the notorious and disgraceful disposal of war surplus property of the U.S. Government: jeeps, Army trucks, Quonset huts, cement, lumber, foodstuffs and the literally millions of items needed to wage a war. It was valued at more than a billion U.S. dollars. Originally meant for the U.S. Armed Forces for the liberation of the Philippines and invasion of Japan, the U.S. Government turned it over to the Philippine Government. Supposedly, they were to be auctioned to the public and the proceeds counted as aid to the Philippines. Such an anomalous scandal of corruption occurred from these materials! It was a disaster waiting to explode!

An outstanding conspiracy involved the cargo of 185,000 cases of beer and other alcoholic beverages on a U.S. freighter anchored in Manila Bay. They were part of the PX recreation supplies destined for the liberation forces. When the war ended abruptly with the dropping of the atomic bombs, it was no longer feasible to keep the supplies since the soldiers were hurriedly returned to the United States.

The editor assigned me to view the auction process of the wine and beer shipment to be held at the U.S. Headquarters on Dewey Boulevard. I was the first reporter on the scene for the bidding at 12 Noon sharp. The only person present and in charge was a Mr. O'Shaughnessy*. After presenting my credentials, I asked, "Where are the closed bids?" No response.

"Are we too early?"

He laughed, "There is no more auction. It was canceled."

In amazement, I queried, "What happened? Did the ship sink suddenly in the bay? Come on! I have to write about it!"

He laughed again, "The bidding was canceled because the goods were awarded to a Mr. Gilberto Francisco,* a friend of the President."

"But it was supposed to be a competitive auction, was it not?" I countered.

"Yeah, yeah! Sure! But, 'His Nibs' called my boss and told him it was awarded to Mr. Gilberto Francisco."*

O'Shaughnessy* revealed that 'His Nibs' was none other than the President of the Philippine Islands, himself! Furthermore, he and his "boss had no control over the situation. And that's that!"

My by-line across the front page that day read:
"HIS NIBS CALLED OFF THE AUCTION OF $200 MILLION
     WORTH OF BEER FLOATING IN MANILA BAY!
     HE AWARDED IT TO MR. GILBERTO FRANCISCO."*
An incredible fortune was made that day!

As a result, several U.S. personnel were hastily transferred. I immediately began to receive threats to my life for the by-line and the published account.

I was also involved in the newspaper revelations and publicity of political corruption regarding several Congressmen engaged in sponsoring refugees from China and Formosa. The "going price" for a Congressional sponsorship of an alien was a $10,000 payoff for each case. The death threats multiplied.

As part of the political fallout, presidential pressure was placed

---

* Name changed to protect identity.

upon the advertisers of our new pro-American new monthly magazine, *The Nation's Advocate*. After only a little more than a year, we were forced to cease publication again. None of the corporations had the backbone to face the anger of Malacanan and be confronted with loss of profits or to be forced out of business. The intimidations increased.

Indeed, the threats continued *even* in Washington, D.C. Late one spring afternoon in 1949, a colonel confronted my husband and me on 14th and G Streets, N.W., and pointed a shiny, short-barreled revolver at us. He warned us not to continue to work for the veterans. However, several people departing from a nearby restaurant interrupted the scene, and he disappeared around the corner and into the National Press Club Building.

The merry-go-round of corruption continued as hundreds of millions of dollars worth of U.S. material were theoretically turned over to the Philippine government and promptly got lost in the shuffling of papers and careers.

Later, following extreme pressures of money, and politics as usual, Malacanan, (the White House of the Philippines), announced a "General Amnesty" to all Japanese collaborators, in fulfillment of a presidential campaign promise.

The problem originated in April 1945, when Manuel Roxas and four other leaders of the Japanese puppet government surrendered to the U.S. Armed Forces near Baguio. General MacArthur proclaimed him to be a liberated patriot; the others were declared Japanese collaborators.

This act of pardon grafted an aura of respectability to the Roxas "persona" as one unjustly accused, whereas in reality, he was a guerrilla forced to serve under duress by the Japanese puppet government.

The U.S. Army had already incarcerated approximately five thousand collaborators.

Roxas made the collaboration issue a major facet of his election campaign against the then President, Sergio Osmena.

Later, as President, he proclaimed an Act of Amnesty which effectively freed thousands of Filipinos and *mestizos* of Spanish and

Chinese lineage. Only at this time, was it revealed to me what had been the underlying purpose of my confinement in the Muntinglupa Prison for female collaborators.

Top echelon guerrilla leaders rightly perceived that since I was a member of the politico-social elite, I would be accepted by the female internees as "one of their own."

During my three weeks behind bars, I constantly mingled with my fellow inmates and observed their behavior and actions.

In the debriefing session, it was recorded how too many of the socially prominent women had sold both their souls and their bodies to the highest-ranking enemy officers and political leaders.

The majority of prisoners had valises or bulging suitcases

Top: **Manuel A. Roxas, First President of Independent Philippines**
Bottom: **Elpidio Quirino, Second President**

crammed with legitimate paper currency. Unbelievably, some had hundreds of millions of genuine pesos fresh from the National Bank of the Philippines.

More importantly, to the Oriental female mentality, were the satchels overflowing with pearl necklaces and gold jewelry as well as loose diamonds, rubies and especially Chinese jade. These and small gold bars were worth infinitely more than paper money.

A few of the women also had wire filaments studded with West Point Academy rings "liberated" from captured or deceased American Army officers.

In the Subic Bay black market at that time, the selling price for Academy rings was $5.00. However, when melted down to bullion it was a much more valuable commodity since it occupied less space and was easily secreted inside one's clothing.

Ah! If only the Army wardens had confiscated these rings, regardless of political fallout, and mailed them to the bereaved relatives and survivors as a final token of closure and honor by the U.S. Army.

With the presidential signing of the Amnesty, all was theoretically forgiven and the collaborators restored to their former places of political and economic authority.

The results of this debacle have persisted throughout Philippine history until today, because it effectively returned members of the ruling *ilustrado* classes to positions of dominance.

When released, quite a few of the women immediately flaunted their newfound freedom with parties given in honor of MacArthur's headquarters staff.

I personally was invited to magnificent gala balls and dinner parties honoring these high-ranking American officers.

In less than two weeks, the women simply transferred their charms and allegiance to become the mistresses of their Army and Navy officer guests.

My three weeks in jail gathering evidence was truly in vain!

It seems that only God in His infinite wisdom will right the wrongs committed in those days!

> REPUBLIC OF THE PHILIPPINES
> DEPARTMENT OF THE INTERIOR
> MANILA
>
> February 26, 1948
>
> TO ALL PROVINCIAL COMMANDERS
> OF CENTRAL LUZON
>
> Mrs. MAMERTA BLOCK, the bearer, is a newspaper-
> woman of the STAR REPORTER. She is going to Central
> Luzon to gather news for her paper. The Secretary
> of the Interior desires that Mrs. Mamerta Block be
> given all courtesies and privileges of the press by
> members of the provincial and municipal officials
> and the municipal police.
>
> ELIAS DIOQUINO
> Lt-Colonel, PC
> Military Adviser &
> Chief, Public Order Div.

Updated "Carte Blanche" Press Pass
(issued to author as investigative journalist)

Chapter 25

ASSASSINATE THE PRESIDENT!

On a scorching hot Sunday morning in the spring (dry season) of 1946, I stopped in a cantina in Cavite for a cola drink and experienced the greatest newspaper and radio scoop I ever had as a journalist.

I unearthed the plot to overthrow the democratic government of the Philippine Islands in a literal bloodbath—to be replaced with a dictatorship by a large and fully armed group of disgruntled and angry guerrilleros—in less than ten days!

It was a reporter's dream assignment!

However, I could not publish it in my column or announce it on my radio program without compromising the confidentiality of the informants. Neither could I jeopardize President Manuel Roxas.

Today, it would probably be a hotly discussed ethical "special case history" or seminar in schools of journalism:

(1) to keep confidences, or

(2) to break trusts, or

(3) to work underground for the "greater good" of the people or a nation

(4) or—to do nothing!

What should a journalist do when she becomes *involved* as an integral part of the story itself?

What should be the course and extent of my actions, *if any*?

It all began so innocently! My Naval officer husband and I were on a Sunday picnic trip in Cavite Province, when we decided to stop at a cantina to obtain some Coca-Colas.

I noticed that while inside, several men had surrounded him in a menacing manner near the bar and were discussing something. Finally, he paid the barkeeper and returned to the jeep. With shaking hands, he offered me the bottle of cola and then blurted out:

"You need to talk to them real fast in Tagalog (the national language). They're a mean band of unrecognized guerrillas. They all have rifles and pistols. It seems like I stumbled into a plot of some kind or other. They acted like I was a secret agent against them. They at least smiled when I mentioned Major Antiporda's unrecognized guerrillas."

I agreed to return and speak to them as a fellow lieutenant in the underground resistance movement.

As we entered the archway, it was a scene reminiscent of a John Wayne movie in a Texas saloon. The only missing artifact was a honky-tonk piano. A handsome, mature Filipino about 5 feet, 8 inches tall, greeted and invited us to enter his humble dwelling and be his guests for Sunday dinner with his guerrilla staff. He was attired in a khaki uniform with a general's stars on the collar lapels. A loaded .45 caliber pistol in an open holster was his sidearm.

Pushing his shiny black hair straight back with both hands, he informed us that he was General Jose Vizcaya,* leader of the guerrillas located in the area.

The tall man by his side, Lt. Colonel Rosario, was his trusted assistant. Two other rugged-looking men served as officers and bodyguards.

At this moment, a dozen other khaki-clad men appeared from the shadows, all armed with rifles or pistols (or both). They joined in the circle to listen.

When we heard him being called Doctor as well as General, he explained that he had been medically trained in Spain and returned to the Philippines to serve his own countrymen. He had a long and successful practice of medicine prior to the outbreak of hostilities with Japan. As a succourer of his fellowmen including those who had resisted the invasion, he was placed on the Japan-

_____

* Name changed to protect identity

ese "Wanted List." Not too long after, a *Makapili* (or Japanese sympathizer) betrayed him. His wife and children were trapped and burned alive in a secret hideaway a few miles south of Manila.

In a spirit of revenge, he increased and intensified his resistance. He became known as a fearless and indefatigable fighter with his guerrilla members against the Japanese. It was only a matter of time before he became an outstanding name on the Japanese "Super-Wanted List." By dint of secrecy and good security, most of his men and their families had survived the Occupation.

After being delayed for more than an hour, the ladies insisted that we have our dinner of rice and Filipino delicacies. Contrary to local Spanish-Filipino custom, there was no traditional siesta after the meal. Instead, General Vizcaya revealed his plans to obtain justice for the widows, wounded and missing-in-action of the Filipino guerrilla fighters, especially those on the island of Luzon. His followers noisily urged him on.

Then it was my turn to respond.

I recounted my efforts in behalf of the Luzon guerrilla movement as a member of Barrion's Division. Emphasizing that I was engaged in counterespionage work, I also had been captured and tortured for two months and twenty-seven days in the infamous Fort Santiago Prison Camp in Intramuros, Manila. My pregnancy brought no leniency. They all nodded knowingly. Many exclaimed, *"Sus!"* and *"Sus Maria!"*

At last, after a final, brutal torture session, I was thrown out as dead and consigned to a mass grave. I kept hearing *"Sus!"* and *"Hindi puede!"*—"May it never happen!" as I spoke.

However, a young medical intern, while playing with his stethoscope discovered that both the baby and I had heartbeats. They immediately rushed me to the Catholic Belgian Nunnery, but the other two bodies were consigned to potter's field. Staring at me they muttered, *"Jesusmariahosep!"*

After my Caesarian delivery of an infant son and a period of convalescence, I resumed my anti-Japanese activities. I had participated in the recapture of Manila with PCAU-4. Later, the U.S. Army denied my guerrilla service and refused to accept my status as a legally recognized veteran since I was a woman and an officer. So, I understood full well what pain and disappointment they were undergoing. I knew from the faces of my fellow-sufferers that they were on my side.

When I sat down, there was a long period of silence. Then and only then did General Vizcaya reveal his systematic plan of action to initiate a rebellion to overthrow the government of the Philippines the following week, and that my story was a good example of why he wanted a radical change. "Status quo" was not for him!

He had at his disposal an inner core of several thousand battle-tested warriors. Plus, another group of guerrillas totaling more than 10,000 men who would follow his leadership under any and all circumstances—even unto death—to improve their native homeland. Patriots one and all!

General Vizcaya was a mature, well-built, solid-looking man with a finely molded figure and rounded face. An intellectual and professional, he had seemingly been to the doorstep of Hell—and returned. Initially embittered by his personal tragedy and family losses, he had emerged with an even greater faith and a burning, unyielding desire to see justice done for the average Filipino.

In order to succeed, he knew that he would become part of the new leadership of a greater, more-just Philippines as it began its era of new nationhood.

He was well aware of the *Hukbalahaps* (agrarian reformers of Central Luzon), and others who had been deprived of their rights and had also become anti-establishment as well as anti—American and pro-Communist. He fully understood their hatred against the absentee landowners and oligarchy and he sympathized with them. They would probably assist him but posed a danger because they were still well armed from their fierce resistance against the Japanese Army. He did not want any internecine guerrilla problems.

The plan was so simple it would probably succeed. To take effect—in less than ten days! That accounted for the tension when we stopped at their headquarters. He thought there had been a "leak" and their cause would be compromised.

General Vizcaya personally would lead the major thrust to surround, isolate and invade Malacanan, the Presidential Compound (or "White House"), near the outskirts of Manila. They would simultaneously blockade the Pasig River access to keep reinforcements at bay and set up armed roadblocks at the arterial crossroads. A second group of followers would take over the Philippine Army compounds' communication and weapons centers and invite the soldiers to join them in the struggle against government corruption.

As a crucial public relations coup, they would expropriate the major radio stations to inform the public of their reasons for overthrowing a corrupt government and ask for their cooperation to usher in the dawn of a true democracy.

Other smaller armed detachments were to seize the dockside area, the Manila Police Station, as well as those in the neighboring provinces.

Taking prisoners was not a priority. If you resisted, you would be shot on the spot, especially collaborators, *Kempeitai* sympathizers, or *Makapilis* (Japanese partisans). They were familiar with the old boxing adage that if the head drops, the body will crumble.

They were aware from the media, and especially the Manila Press, that much of the citizenry felt cheated, ignored and left out as the new government was moving ahead in jerks and starts into yet more corruption.

President Manuel Roxas, they contended, was not a true guerrilla but rather a minion of the U.S. Army leadership; and that General Douglas MacArthur had desired, assisted and maneuvered his presidential campaign. President Roxas was expendable and would be shot when he resisted!

Another bitter gripe centered on the Presidential Order of Amnesty for elite socialites, the oligarchy, men and women who had been Japanese collaborators.

If it were to be the "same old story of graft and corruption" as the country embarked on its hard-won freedom, they would be left out completely. Recent corrupt elections, they said, had proven that point.

There were no substantial plans for the southern island of Mindanao and only a makeshift structure for the central Visayan area with the exception of one top guerrilla leader, General Peralta, whom they trusted. They recognized that by controlling Luzon and Manila, the capital, the rest of the country would follow as they explained their cause on the radio and in the press.

They discerned that their cry of justice and honor for the common patriotic *tao* (or Mr. Average Citizen) would rally the hearts and souls of the great majority of their countrymen. And they were willing to hazard their lives once again for the beloved "Pearl of the Orient."

My husband and I sat in stunned silence. There was no doubt in my mind that as a proven man of action, the general would do exactly what he said.

The President would be assassinated!

A new government proclaimed and installed—with General Vizcaya as the initial President/Dictator!

As General Vizcaya paused, he was applauded with many *Mabuhay!'s* and *El Presidente!'s* by his followers who now overflowed the main room.

But, fortunately they were soon silenced when I stood up and again exhorted:

"Gentlemen, like you, I was active during the past three years as a G-2 Intelligence Officer with 'Barrion's Division'—a Guerrilla Fighting Unit. I *also* suffered and lost loved ones, but you *must* know the truth. I personally know that only the Truth shall free us from hatred, anger and indignation. First, I can assure you that President Roxas acted like a true guerrilla and a secret commander during the Japanese Occupation.

"General de Jesus, a West Point graduate, before the Japanese captured him and he 'disappeared' permanently, received secret messages from Roxas; and I took those messages from his hands and delivered and circulated them among the various guerrilla outfits. To prove this point, all you have to do is contact some people that you know personally such as General Peralta, Colonel Dikit, Major Antiporda and Colonel Santos—all true guerrilla fighters." The audience became especially still and silent at the mention of this roll call of heroes.

"Also, my own Commander, Colonel Barilea, was ordered by President Roxas to seize a radio transmitter in Nasugbu enabling us to receive and transmit news and messages to Australia.

"Your best bet is to petition the President, even if you're not sure of him, to intervene with the PhilRyCom (Philippine-Ryuku Command) Recognition Team of the U.S. Army to grant you fairness and justice. We can go to the United States President, the U.S. Congress; and I am sure we will be given a fair hearing. All of us believe in the democratic process. Let us give America a chance to do the right thing. As the late President Roosevelt said, 'All of those Filipinos, loyal to Democracy, fighting with America, will be compensated for their sacrifices.' Let us continue to believe in America's altruism.

"We as a nation," I continued, "were promised our independence in 1946. Let us not scuttle our chances now. A little patience and trust in the fairness and justice of our cause, by true friends in both our government and the United States government, will help us succeed.

"Gentlemen, let us all join, with the thousands of veterans, recognized or not, to a common cause. Bring your petition to the American public so they can urge the U.S. Congress to act for us. Last, let us pray and ask God Almighty to help us all with our just endeavor."

When I sat down there was a mighty round of applause and simultaneous cheers of *Mabuhay*! But, again the guards outside remonstrated with us that we should be quiet so that the neighbors would not be aware of their actions.

The future of the entire Philippine Islands resided in the hearts and minds of this elite corps of guerrilla warriors!

General Vizcaya was a true example of the idealistic Filipino *romantico* with outstanding emotional and oratorical skills.

Although a professional and intellectual, he had an innate sense of compassion for the common man and wanted him to succeed in his service to family, country and humanity.

The major difficult area of decision in arranging for a renewed society was apparent in the ancient provincial proverb "All things are settled in blood!"

Once the revolution had removed the undesirable collaborators and traitors, the new government would prosper and flourish.

A dreamer, planner and idealist—he seemed unable to contemplate or micromanage on a day-to-day basis much beyond the initial takeover period.

If the Vizcaya Army had succeeded, then the great American ideals of democracy would have collapsed.

The world nations would have mocked and derided the United States of America when it failed in managing its colonial enterprise.

It is inherent in the Filipino nature and custom to react not only with the emotions but to seek logical solutions to their problems.

After a lengthy discussion, General Vizcaya and his inner circle voted to give democracy another chance.

As a result, the planned revolution was temporarily aborted until there was a special meeting with President Roxas.

The scene in the semi-darkened hall was reminiscent of the Homeric sagas where groups of warriors had open discussions and reached reasonable conclusions.

Early the next morning, I was whisked into the Executive Office of the President in Malacanan, accompanied by my editor; the Presidential Secretary; my commander, Colonel Dominador Barilea; and several other prominent guerrilla leaders. The President and Colonel Barilea were personal friends since childhood and on a first-name basis.

President Roxas arose from behind the imposing presidential desk and greeted us warmly. He remembered me from the prewar days as a reporter/columnist. Then, we all sat down in a circle around him.

I briefed him on the details of the preceding day.

President Roxas was caught completely by surprise, being both astounded and impressed. The President immediately swore us unto absolute secrecy and *never* to reveal what had happened that morning. *Nothing* was to be published nor broadcast! There were to be *no* "leaks." It was imperative that we should *not* in any way jeopardize the future of our democracy and nation. Realizing the high stakes and that our nationhood was "on the line," we all agreed to abide by this decision.* President Roxas would summon General Vizcaya to his office within the next twenty-four hours.

As his first appointment of the day, he invited General Vizcaya to Malacanan for a conference. President Roxas promised to take immediate action to alleviate as many of the problems as best as he could.

Before he was able to fully implement his program, President Roxas died suddenly of a massive heart attack/stroke while delivering a speech at the U.S. Clark Field in Pampanga Province.

Vice President Elpidio Quirino, who succeeded him in office, also took up the interests of the veterans. He and the then Secretary of Interior Mr. Jose Zuleta, both gave their official and public support to bring about a better national understanding regarding the unrecognized veterans and their dependents and survivors.

This in turn led to the organization of The Filipino Guerrilla Veterans Legion. They later presented a formal petition to Thomas Lockett, Charge d'Affaires of the U.S. Embassy in Manila.

Both the Philippine Veterans Legion and the Filipino Guerrilla Veterans Legion in a combined mass public meeting elected me to represent them before the U.S. Congress and The Department of the Army. Instruction was given to present their petition to President Harry S. Truman.

---

* Revealed only for the first time with the publication of this book.

Author exhorting Guerrilla leaders prior to departure on mission to USA
(left to right) **Col. Macam, Isaac Block, author, Col. Dikit, Col. Pamintuan**

Chapter 26

ON TO WASHINGTON, D.C.

During the latter months of 1947 and throughout most of 1948, local "news" and rumors traveled faster than truth in Greater Manila regarding the plight of the many World War II widows and orphans and how and where they could obtain help, sustenance and justice.

Our home served as a way station for innumerable claimants. Some of them came from the Visayan Islands and distant Mindanao to U.S. Army Headquarters in Manila. Most of them arrived with no place to stay for several nights or weeks. Others came to Manila with only the fare for the trip itself, let alone money for food. "Homelessness" is not a new word to the Filipinos. When we were able, we shared our limited resources with them, especially our food. For barefoot widows, we purchased cheap wooden shoes called *bakia* and ready-made dresses.

Filipino Army veteran claimants as well as Philippine Scouts, guerrillas and widows were confused with the infinite paper requirements such as birth certificates, proof of service, proper affidavits, genuine duplicates, notary seals, tax and revenue stamps, etc. required by a government consumed with the idea of red tape—red tape taken to the extreme.

Two vivid examples of hard-heartedness and injustice received wide media publicity:

VET GOES MAD!

"Insanity, as a result of receiving a backpay check for 97 centavos caused the death of Sergeant Ariston Y. Almalel of Binan, Laguna, last March 15, it was established the other day by the physician who conducted the autopsy on the dead soldier according to Lorenzo G. Almeda, a surgeon from Herbosa, Tondo.

"Almalel, a Bataan veteran, believed that because of his long service in the Philippine Army Medical Corps, he would receive a big sum representing his backpay, Almeda said. But on February 5, he received a PNB check for P.97 and immediately went insane."

SLAIN HERO'S PARENTS GET P.58 CHECK

"A check for P.58 representing the death benefit of their son, Meliton was received by Agapito Baladadia and his wife from the Finance Service.

"Meliton was killed in action at Barrio Ganiogan, this town, March 1945, when a reconnaissance patrol of Marking's Fil-American troops engaged a retreating column of Japanese soldiers and *Makapilis*.

"The accompanying letter sent by registered mail informed the couple that each parent was entitled to 29 centavos each."

When their countless pages of documentation were in order, we often accompanied the claimants to the offices of the U.S. Army Claims Division. It was a great boost when authentic claims were published in my column in *The Star Reporter*. I interviewed others on my weekly program on Radio KZPI for the Philippine Veterans Legion.

As the unrecognized guerrilla situation deteriorated into unlawfulness, in October 1948, a preliminary meeting of more than 500 key men gathered in the Samanillo Building for a strategy and planning session.

Then, the Philippine Veterans Legion and the Filipino Guerrilla Veterans Legion held a combined, gigantic street rally at the Quiapo Square, Manila, during the last week of October 1948. Led by the newly elected Congressman Ramon Magsaysay, the mass meeting elected me to be the chairman to head the mission for the Philippine veterans to the United States Congress and to the President of the United States. A petition and legal documentation were prepared. There was to be a public portrayal of the plight of the half-million starving veterans, widows, orphans and jobless veterans who fought unselfishly with Americans to help win World War II in the Far East.

Later, at a mammoth rally held at the American Embassy on October 29, 1948, a similar petition to be forwarded to the President of the United States and the Secretary of the Army was presented to Mr. Thomas Lockett, Charge d'Affaires. Finally—it was received by the Secretary of State on "12/06/48" and by the Secretary of the Army on "12/09/48." Widespread media coverage plus Philippine congressional and judicial representatives flooded the Presidential Palace.

Elpidio Quirino, who became President upon the death of President Manuel Roxas, summoned my husband and me to Malacanan Palace. Surrounded by high-ranking officialdom and standing in front of the magnificent presidential desk, he announced that he would present to me a roundtrip airplane ticket to Washington, D.C. While the photographers' bulbs kept flashing, he, possibly seeking the veterans' votes, repeated again and again, "I *will* support Mrs. Block's mission! I *will* support Mrs. Block's mission!"

The MANILA CHRONICLE

MANILA, PHILIPPINES, SUNDAY, DECEMBER 19, 1948   No. 212

AID FOR GUERRILLA MISSION—Mrs. Mamerta Black, member of a two-man mission of unrecognized Philippine guerrillas and veterans to the United States, recently received from SPC Chairman Jose C. Zulueta (left photo) the sum of P2,500 as his personal contribution to the funds of the mission. At right photo can be seen Mrs. Black receiving from President Quirino a round-trip ticket to the U. S. and presidential blessings. Mrs. Black recently left for abroad on a PAL plane.

Newspaper photo shows President Quirino presenting round-trip ticket to United States to author.

Once more, I had to leave my family and children to heed the call of duty, as I saw it, to my country and for the welfare of my people.

The Veterans Legions, according to Philippine custom, entrusted me to bestow their gift of a beautiful, full-length, Philippine-designed *Saya* or butterfly-sleeved dress woven from finely textured and delicate pineapple fiber to Mrs. Bess Truman.

My two-year-old daughter, Aida, accompanied me in what was then a four-day trip to Washington, D.C.

On December 6, 1948, several hundred veterans from the combined Filipino Guerrilla Veterans Legion and Philippine Veterans Legion gathered at the Manila Airport. They pledged their continuing allegiance and support of our mission to Washington as we departed on the first leg of the journey.

Our last warm weather stop was in Hawaii.

As the airplane was preparing to descend at Oakland Airport, the steward came to my seat and volunteered, "I will help you with this pretty little girl, Aida. Let me have your coats, please."

"What coats?" I asked.

"You mean you are going on a mission to America in December and you do not have winter coats?"

"That's just about it, I suppose," I replied. "Nobody, much less my American husband, warned me about winter coats or anything of that kind."

"But, Mrs. Block, you will freeze," the steward shuddered.

Shrugging my shoulders, I remarked, "Oh well, the Lord will take care of us."

When he repeated this statement to the stewardess, I observed that he pointed his finger to his head, made circular motions and whispered, "She's lost her marbles."

However, he quickly grabbed some blankets, gave one to me, wrapped another around my daughter and then escorted us from the plane to the airport waiting room.

As soon as he opened the swinging doors to the VIP Lounge, we had a great surprise. Walking toward us were our old Manila friends, Colonel Edward Lansdale, two other Army officers and their wives. They recently had been transferred to their new base at The Presidio, Monterey, California. Each of the wives carried a coat on her arm. Remembering the tender age of my daughter, Aida, Mrs. Lansdale had brought the correct size for her. The problem was with my size. Being exactly five feet tall, I could not fit into a size ten. The steward's bulging eyes were awed at what the Lord had accomplished that day with three coats on such short notice.

Colonel Lansdale, later promoted to Major General, led pacification programs in the Philippine Islands as well as in Viet Nam. They were truly "beautiful Americans."

When we landed at the Washington National Airport four days before Christmas, my mother-in-law, Mrs. Joseph Block and her daughter, Charlotte, greeted us. They invited us to visit them in Baltimore, Maryland, until the United States Congress convened in January 1949. This became an opportunity to meet and know my husband's relatives. My daughter began her first lessons in English from her paternal grandfather. Her total English vocabulary was in response to three questions:

(1) "What is your name, little girl?"
(2) "How old are you?"
(3) "Where do you live?"

Grandpa Block, very patiently, escorted her through every room in the house and introduced her to the names of all the household items we take for granted. She quickly learned: door, doorknob, key, keyhole, hinge, lock, open, close, in, out, turn, right, left, up, down, middle, etc. In less than two weeks, she was bilingual!

There was, however, a minor language misunderstanding. Arriving home one evening, I observed that my mother-in-law was upset and accused Aida of referring to her meal as "slop."

My husband countered that she had never heard that word in her entire young life. It was determined that both the delicious dinner of chicken pot pie and coconut-topped yellow cake were designated as slop.

I requested "Mother Block" to serve her another small helping of each item as we ate our own supper.

My daughter enthusiastically devoured the "seconds." As her fork sank into the meal she chattered, "Mmmmmmh! *Ma-sa-rrap! Ma-sa-rrap!*" Mother Block's face became solemn, "That's *just* what she said earlier! It's slop!"

I explained, "Your granddaughter is trying to tell you, 'Mmm-mmmh!—*Ma-sa-rrap! Ma-sa-rrap!*'—that's *so* tasty! So delicious!' in the Philippine language. Just look at her facial expression as she devours the food—*that* tells the story!"

Mother Block learned a new word that day and we understood how difficult it can be to translate different languages. And all went well, as Grandpa Block continued with her English lessons room by room, but with special attention to the—kitchen!

Since my new relatives were lifelong residents of Maryland, it was a fortuitous opportunity to seek aid from Senator Tydings, especially since he was also the co-sponsor of the Tydings-McDuffie Act, granting independence to the Philippine Islands. In addition, he served as a member of the Committee on Armed Services. Preliminary appointments were made.

One hour before the Joint Session of the United States Congress on January 3, 1949, I entered the office of Senator Millard E. Tydings.

With a size ten coat engulfing my ninety-four-pound frame, I must have looked like "The Wreck of the Hesperus." The secretary just stared at me.

Timidly, I announced, "I am Mrs. Block from the Philippines. I have an appointment with Senator Tydings."

"Well," she finally responded, "I am not sure he has time to see you. Today is the Joint Session of Congress. Have a seat."

I sat glumly on the chair facing the inner door to the Senator's office and started to pray for heavenly help.

Suddenly, the inner door swung open and a very tall, middle-aged man with a kindly expression looked in my direction. Extending his arm, he said, "You must be Mrs. Block, the Philippine Guerrilla leader. Come in."

My papers were ready and complete with the details of the

Daughter Aida: "No hablo Americano."

purpose and function of my mission. He was surprised and attentive to my orderly presentation of the petition for the Philippine veterans. After briefly scrutinizing the complete file, he called his secretary and dictated a letter to the Secretary of National Defense, The Honorable James Forrestal. He instructed me to deliver the letter to the Pentagon and insisted that I return to his office after my interview with the Armed Forces at the Pentagon.

The next day, I went to the office of the Secretary of National Defense and presented the letter of Senator Tydings and the petition of the Philippine/Guerrilla Veterans Legion. This was later verified by a Secretary of Defense document dated January 15, 1949, that I was interviewed at the office of the Secretary of National Defense and delivered Senator Tydings' letter "as well as the Resolution in thereto which petitions the President 'to ask Congress to pass legislation that will permit the reexamination of all existing *bona fide* claims for recognition, etc.' "

Senator Tydings' letter was the door-opener to further developments.

It soon became all too apparent that the offices of the Secretary of Defense and the Army were quite unhappy that the entire case might be reopened. Subsequent adverse publicity might possibly stain careers for those who might have been guilty of guerrilla recognition improprieties.

Our documentation clearly displayed how entire guerrilla units had been stripped from official Army records and the empty spaces in the original papers had been substituted with fake and illegal units.

The evidence showing these replacements was overwhelming. A central test case involved Colonel Mario Pamintuan's HQ Northwest Pampanga Military District—"NWPMD." The *prima facie* evidence was so vivid and straightforward that it was impossible not to conclude that they had been deliberately removed and exchanged by high-ranking officials in the claims section of the U.S. Army PhilRyCom (Philippine-Ryuku Command) Headquarters, located in the Manila area.

When apprised of these actions, Major General George F.

Moore, who inherited the problem as the PhilRyCom commander, attempted to take a remedial and appropriate response, but was limited by an "expiration date" over which he had no control. He was sympathetic, but stated that the problem had to be resolved back in Washington, D.C., because of the termination date for guerrilla recognition.

As the Philippine/Guerrilla Veterans petition touched base in the various committees and offices, it became listed on their letters as a "famous case!" They then began the "big stall" which lasted most of the winter and into the spring.

The daily commuting by train from Baltimore to Washington, in below-freezing weather, became as discouraging as the progress of our slowed-down claims.

Although I was delighted to walk through early snowstorms and watch my daughter build her first snowman, I was not really a winter sports fan with my tropical upbringing.

I resolved that my husband, who was caring for the other children in Manila, should come and provide assistance in making the rounds of offices on Capitol Hill. Consequently, he left our sons, Florentino and Peter, with my relatives in Manila and joined me at his own expense in the continuing struggle to help the Philippine veterans' cause. Arriving in Washington, D.C. in a white Palm Beach suit on a snowy day, his first major purchase was a winter suit and overcoat.

Mr. Ambler of Virginia, longtime Service Officer of the Veterans of Foreign Wars in Washington, D.C., arranged for me to speak at several VFW state conventions and suggested we hire a public relations firm. The International News Service drafted plans for publicity with a few favorable results. Various speakers' agencies also arranged several promising opportunities. My initial invitation was a ten-minute speech in the Statler Hilton in Washington at the convention of The Grand Army of the Republic. A charming matron introduced me to her daughter, Miss Ella Harlee, who later became one of my dearest friends in Washington.

Miss Harlee, a member of The National Press Club, worked as the public relations officer for The Federation of Churches. She was also an account executive for a nationally syndicated radio and television religious program broadcasting from American University.

When she discovered that I was a *pro bono* speaker for veterans' recognition, she confided, "Mamerta, you will have more opportunities if you speak in churches, for many churches have members who are veterans. They can help you approach public officials to lobby unofficially for your cause."

Within a few days I had my second engagement, speaking to the adult Sunday School class of the New York Avenue Presbyterian Church where I met its dynamic pastor, Reverend Peter Marshall. Some of the visitors, members of other denominations, soon sent letters requesting me to address their own United Methodist Churches in Washington, Northern Virginia, and Maryland.

Two months later, Mrs. Dorothy Long, President of the Washington, D.C., Baptist Women's Missionary Union, took me under her wing. She made arrangements in many Baptist churches for me to recount my experiences demonstrating how God had sustained and enabled me to survive during the war.

I also was guest speaker at various meetings of the Lions Club, Rotary Club, The Inner Wheel, DAR (Daughters of the American Revolution), Gold Star and Blue Star Mothers, Kiwanis, etc.

After missing a train connection from Macon, Georgia, Miss Lolla Rooke requested me to be the guest speaker of her women's class at the Baptist Tabernacle of Atlanta. I observed that one well-dressed sophisticated woman was spellbound as I related my wartime experiences. After my concluding remarks, she raised her hand and came forward. Miss Rooke then revealed that this lady was her dear friend, Mrs. Margaret Mitchell, author of *Gone With the Wind*.

The next day Miss Rooke and I were invited to the Mitchell home for a light brunch of chicken sandwiches, cake, coffee and conversation. Mrs. Mitchell thanked me again for sharing my experience and confided to Miss Rooke that she had made a life-changing commitment to Jesus as Lord that very day.

While driving to the train station, Miss Rooke gave me a beautiful leather-bound Bible as a farewell gift.

What a shock to read several months later that Mrs. Mitchell had been killed in an automobile accident!

Meanwhile, my husband left no stone unturned on follow-up actions and personal interviews. During the same time, he and I prepared innumerable packets, brochures, status papers and publicity regarding our progress. I appeared before the Veterans Affairs Committees of the Senate and House of Representatives, subcommittees, legal office of the Secretary of Defense, etc.

Chapter 27

A DISAPPOINTING EMBASSY

The worst handicap to the mission was my own Embassy of the Philippines. The Philippine culture of those days was for women to play the role of second-class citizens.

"A woman is only a woman!" was the male-dominated theme. In other words, they should stay home, attend church, bear children, embroider fine linen, be social butterflies (if wealthy), and surely be an adornment of her husband's life and home. It was similar to the old medieval phrase: *Kuchen, Kindern, Kirchen*—a platitude that reflects a mentality long since vanished, but not in the Philippines with its Spanish heritage. This theme of subservience was continued by the Philippine Embassy, even in Washington, D.C.

I was judged guilty of being a woman doing a man's work!

Written communications with the Ambassador, or the Counselor, in the Washington office was the primary contact I had with current events of guerrilla affairs in Manila. Inexplicably, they were antagonistic to the mission for the betterment of their own countrymen!

The same scenario occurred again and again: I would telephone the embassy and make an appointment to see the Ambassador. The Counselor would inform me that I should be at the embassy at a certain date and time. I followed his directions explicitly. However, when I arrived, I was always notified that the Ambassador had left a few minutes prior to my appearance for an official and/or other appointment.

In addition, the embassy usually dispersed the Philippine/Guerrilla Veterans Legion monetary funds, donated sacrificially by the veterans back home, for the expenses of gasoline, travel, paper work, telephone bills, etc. But, it was always late and was under duress. We were made to feel that we were not worthy to receive it.

At last, we received a letter from Colonel Manuel T. Dikit, Commander of the Philippine Veterans Legion, that President Quirino had promised to send financial aid to the embassy to be authorized from his discretionary funds. But after only $2,000 was disbursed to my associate Colonel Pamintuan for his personal expenses, we were left unpaid. We soon became unable to pay our obligations and were sued by various creditors. By March, 1951, things had so deteriorated that my husband was forced to pay personally the veterans' bills by court order of the District of Columbia.

Our progress was also greatly hindered when several vital letters from Senator Tydings and the Secretary of Defense were conveniently "lost."

Chapter 28

UP—DOWN—UP

After almost five months of making the rounds on Capitol Hill, Senator Tydings called me to his office and summarized, "Young woman, I believe your work for the Philippine veterans has finally paid off." He gave me a copy of the letter of recommendation from Mr. Draper, Secretary of the Army, to the State Department. "This declaration means that it is up to your government to take over the negotiations with the U.S. Government. It's now on a government-to-government basis. This signifies that your work is successfully completed."

I thanked him for all the kindness and support he had given to the cause of the Philippine veterans. As I stood to depart he advised, "So now you will confer with your embassy. You did a tremendous job for the Philippine veterans. God bless you!"

Seated on the trolley car of those days, en route to the train station for the daily commute, my thoughts returned to the past months of struggle to obtain our objective—to finally convince the departments of the Army and Defense and some members of Congress of the just cause and claims of the guerrilla veterans, and their widows and orphans. In a moment of time I seemed to relive my first winter in America, with the endless rounds of meetings with various veterans committees, subcommittees, veterans organizations, etc.; irregular mealtimes and the subsequent gnawing hunger eased by fast food restaurant fare such as hot dogs and baked beans; the long hours of commuting from Baltimore to Washington. Then came tears of joy!

I thanked God for His guidance in all my efforts that had finally come to fruition in assuring that half a million orphans, widows and underground guerrilla veterans who had sacrificed so much for the dream of freedom and independence were now at the threshold of VICTORY!

Alas! My joy was short-lived.

A few weeks later, the Philippine Ambassador summoned me to his office and snickered, "Since your work, with the help of your husband, for the Philippine Veterans Legion claims will now be settled between the United States and Philippine Governments, your work is finished. Your presence is no longer necessary here."

"Shall I now return to my waiting children left with our relatives?"

"Not so," according to the documented reply from Malacanan Palace. "We do not have any more airplane tickets for *your* kind! Besides, we did not ask your husband to come to Washington to help you with the mission. Goodbye and Good Luck! *Adios!*"

I could not believe that the same president who sent us on a mission would renege on sending the other half of my airline ticket to return home! Only Machiavelli's *Prince* would understand their tortured thinking!

It was quite obvious that my two children, six and eight years old, were now sacrificed and forced to wait for their parents to earn enough to purchase the airline tickets. This was in addition to being forced to pay off all the outstanding veterans' bills that the mission incurred.

This curt dismissal of the guerrilla mission five months later was a harsh personal blow.

Never—to this day—have I received even one word of encouragement or thanks from the Embassy. It seemed as if I were expendable as the soldiers who were trapped on Bataan.

Now we concentrated on obtaining funds for the airplane tickets to bring our two sons to the United States. However, after two years of paying off major veterans' bills, we had been able to save only $100 from our salaries toward the $1,000 needed for the airfare.

My husband worked two part-time jobs while completing his Bachelor of Science degree under the G.I. bill.

Contributing to our finances, I taught classes part-time at Miss Alice Keith's National Broadcasting Academy in Washington, D.C. I also was able to audit a class that aided in my "broadcast presence." Many present-day radio and television broadcasters and personalities were my fellow students there. It was a heady atmosphere; but I retain my Spanish-Filipino accent until today.

In addition, I was employed by the Disabled Veterans of America offices as a paper collator at $1.25 per hour.

When our airplane tickets savings were still under $150, Miss Keith and Miss Harlee initiated a crusade to fly the two young children to Washington as soon as possible.

Meanwhile, Miss Keith had introduced me to her sister and

Philippine Mother, Sons Reunited Here

[Times-Herald Photo]

A Philippines wartime guerrilla leader was reunited with her two sons at National Airport last night after three years of separation. The boys, Florentino Blanco, 11, and his brother Pedro, 8, were greeted by their mother, Mrs Mamerta Blanco Block, widowed by the death of the boys' father during the Japanese invasion of the Philippines. Also welcoming the boys were their stepfather and sister, Isaac Block and Aida, 5. Picture shows Florentine, Mrs. Block, Aida and Pedro in order.

brother-in-law, Mr. and Mrs. Rene and Winifred Pinto of Virginia who volunteered to assist us. They advanced the payment for the airfare with the proviso that we pay them back.

Later on, when it was half paid, they canceled the remainder of the bill. We shall never forget them and their generosity for as long as we live!

Senator Kenneth S. Wherry of Nebraska was instrumental in cutting the "red tape" of acquiring passports and visas.

Our family was finally reunited on September 17, 1951, at the Washington National Airport!

Tortured Heroine Rejoins Sons and War Drama Ends

BY HECTOR McLEAN

Weeping with delight and relief, a husky-voiced heroine of war in the Philippines was reunited here last night with two sons she hadn't seen for nearly three years.

The boys, Florentino Blanco, 11, and his brother Pedro, 8, arrived wide-eyed and tongue-tied at National airport aboard American Airlines flight 48 from San Francisco. They had left Manila Friday aboard a Pan-American Airways plane for the flight to the coast.

Their mother, Mrs. Mamerta Blanco Block, who lives in College Park with her husband, Isaac, and their daughter Aida, 5, told their story—and hers—as she nervously awaited the overdue flight.

Flees to the Hills

She gave birth to Pedro in October, 1942, she recalled, 28 hours after her Japanese jailers in Manila had filled out a death certificate for her and thrown her on a growing heap of corpses outside Ft. Santiago.

The boys' father, Pedro Blanco, publisher of the magazine Commonwealth Advocate, had died six months before of wounds suffered in escaping from the Bataan death march.

Blanco's widow fled to the hills with her older son and helped organize one of the first underground movements. Three months later, while operating as a guerrilla courier, she was caught and thrown into a 4 by 3 foot cell.

She displayed her hands as she told of "questioning" by her Japanese captors. The scar under the nail of her left thumb, she said, was made by a burning cigar. "But they couldn't make me talk," she

added, "even tho their torture left scars over all my body."

After three months she lapsed into coma and the Japanese decided she was dead. Friends got her to a hospital and then helped her escape after Pedro was born.

In 1945 Mrs. Blanco met and married Isaac Block, then a Navy lieutenant (j.g.) stationed at Subic bay.

Eyes Glued to Clock

As she talked last night, petite and trim in a dark blue suit, Mrs. Block had eyes only for the airport clock. Aida, bright-eyed with excitement, talked easily with strangers about her fifth birthday last February. Her father, an employe of the veterans administration who was graduated from the University of Maryland last June, quietly filled in the details of their efforts to bring Florentino and Pedro to the United States.

Block and his wife came back to the States in Dec. 1948 on behalf of the Filipino guerrilla veterans, seeking about $100,000,000 compensation for the claims of veterans and their widows. They brought Aida with them, but left the boys in school.

Friends Come to Aid

Their mission completed, the Blocks found themselves stranded here. Block returned to college and they are living now in the veterans' family units at the university—and they decided to bring the boys here.

After a number of difficulties over visa quotas, they won the assistance of several Washington church people.

Sen. Wherry (R) of Nebraska finally eased their immigration problems. The boys' arrival, Mrs. Block said fervently, was "the answer of our prayer to God."

As the big, four-engined plane rolled up, Florentino and Pedro were at a rear window waving wildly. They came marching slowly down the ramp, restrained from running by a stewardess' firm grip on their arms . . . back to their mother and security.

Chapter 29

THE HOUSE ON NINETEENTH STREET

When the United States Army informed Mr. And Mrs. Watson and Lois Owens of College Park, Maryland, that their only son had been killed in the Korean War, they determined that his love for all peoples and desire for world peace would not be in vain. They used the proceeds of his government life insurance policy as seed money to establish a House of Peace in Washington, D.C. They reasoned that since there was a War Department, there should likewise be a Department of Peace to influence our government leaders.

The concept became reality with the incorporation and purchase of the House on Cedar Street in Northwest Washington, D.C. However, it was years ahead of its time. With a lack of funding and publicity, it did not flourish during the era of McCarthyism and the beginning of "The Cold War." When the Board of Directors was obliged to close its doors within several years, the money was placed in escrow for a future attempt.

Simultaneously, Dr. Glenn Clark, author, professor and athletic coach at Macalester College, St. Paul, Minnesota, and a few other leaders had established a series of summer camps in the eastern U.S.A. called the C.F.O., or Camps Farthest Out. They endeavored, as they understood it, to live the Gospel so that it could be experienced in the 20th century. They attempted to pattern their lives in response to the question: "What would the Master do in this specific situation?" All peoples were invited to participate and share.

As the camps increased in number and size, other leaders began a spinoff organization entitled "Koinonia," from the Greek word for "Fellowship" or "Communion." A country estate was purchased north of Baltimore, and a community of like-minded members took up residence to show how dedicated believers could live and perhaps change the lifestyle of America in a small, but tangible way. Again, all were welcome to share in these ideals.

Later Frank Laubach, "the apostle to the illiterate," based his international headquarters there.

My personal memories of Mr. Laubach extended back to childhood when he had been a guest at our rice plantation in Nueva Ecija Province. My father had invited him to stay with us and use our home as his staging center while he journeyed across the Philippines.

It was during those years that Mr. Laubach had perfected his "Each One Teach One" concept of instructing illiterates to learn their own alphabets and then to read. Today, it is recognized by many authorities as a primary teaching tool. Innumerable governments had invited him and his disciples to help raise the literacy rates of their countries.

It was difficult to reconcile my childhood memories of jumping on his knees and being cuddled in his lap after a lapse of so many years. However, he especially remembered my father and his struggle to gain independence for the Philippines from the Spanish.

The Board of Directors of Koinonia, Mr. Laubach, Mrs. Jessie Wickwire Overholt of Indiana, and several others changed the focus of the Owens' dream to what became known as "The House On Nineteenth Street." A down payment was soon made on a four-story residence at 1707 Nineteenth Street, N.W. (at the corner of "R" Street) in Washington, D.C., near the upscale Dupont Circle. Its stated purpose was to be an experiment in international living, as "A Home Away From Home for Foreign Guests With a Spiritual Atmosphere." The doors were open to peoples of all races, colors, religions and backgrounds.

The initial success was short-lived because of a lackadaisical management style leading to excess expenses and a shortage of paying guests. When it was almost bankrupt, Reverend Ward B. Hurlburt, Pastor of Brookland Baptist Church in Washington, D.C., and President of the Board of the House, requested my husband and me to be co-directors and for our family to live on the premises in an attempt to rejuvenate the house. Upon arrival, a week later, in September 1954, the treasurer looked us up and down and sarcastically informed us that:

(1) we had only $48 left in the bank account;

(2) that we were the wrong ones for the job; and

(3) predicted we would not succeed.

He snapped the account book shut and departed. The only paying guest was a twenty-something young man, Ko Asano, of Nisei heritage. We adopted him informally as a member of our family until he moved out of state.

It would have been an impossible situation without the salary of my husband who worked as a science and remedial teacher struggling among the underprivileged in the inner city of Washington, D.C.

We retained the functioning, but old-fashioned kitchen and dining room on the first floor and added a small office and sitting room at the entrance. The central feature of the second floor and the House was a large interdenominational chapel for all peoples in addition to a huge library with a diverse collection of books.

The top two floors became the personal living quarters for guests. We retained two rooms on the third floor for our own family. This personal, family living space was practical since the front windows and mini-balcony could be utilized as an observation post because they overlooked the entrance area. Our children were eager to move into the city. However, it meant a complete change of lifestyle from the suburbs and adjustments to new schools, making friends, recreation, etc.

As a non-profit charitable organization, we turned all monies into the treasury. Rents were at a minimal level and the meals were at cost. After three or four years, we received a monthly stipend of

$50.

Beyond normal rental payments there were only two general rules:

(1) No alcoholic beverages permitted in the residence; and

(2) No one of the opposite sex was permitted in a guest's room unless the guests were married to each other.

I prepared and served breakfast from 8:00 a.m. to 9:00 a.m. and the evening meal from 5:30 to 6:30 p.m. All guests were welcome to dine as members of our family.

Also, the interdenominational chapel was open for meetings, meditation and prayer on a 24-hour basis.

Since the rentals amounted to only about two-thirds of the budget, the Board mailed out an annual Christmas appeal for funds. Fewer than five hundred people nationwide contributed small amounts from $1 and up. This annual event helped to balance the budget. We had no funds to support a mass mailing even on a regional basis. We just thanked God for those contributors who had caught a vision and desired to have a small part in making the Brotherhood of Man a reality, even on a small scale.

Our aim was to have as many nations as possible mix together under one roof and live harmoniously as brothers and sisters in a miniature one-worldwide community of love and respect. We focused on international leaders who were training in the U.S.A.

The guests were sent to us by various agencies of the United States Government: The State Department; Department of Agriculture; AID (Agency for International Development; FAO (Food and Agriculture Organization), UNESCO, etc. Sometimes, we had twenty nations represented in one week. At other times, everybody was from one country such as Zaire, Japan, Philippines, Norway, Iran, etc.

When Washington, D.C. was completely segregated, we were the only institution of its type in the entire metropolitan area that would accept people from African countries.

Many times we were the "Court of Last Resort," when the State Department or Department of Agriculture could not persuade any hotel or boarding house to accept a person who appeared to be a

Negro! We never turned anybody away because of religion or color.

After awhile, our neighborhood knew what we were attempting to do, on a non-profit basis, and it was marvelous to see people of varying skin color garbed in their multicolored native costumes, walking from the House to their places of work or study, speaking a multitude of languages!

But, where and how does one begin?

The family cooperated with stripping, washing, clearing and scrubbing as much of the building as possible. We only had time to paint a few rooms before we opened for business.

On Monday, the children left for their respective schools, my husband went to teach, and I was left to think which chore to tackle first. I concluded, "Since most hotel guests get their initial impression upon entering the lobby, I should make the entrance presentable first." So, I walked several blocks to our neighborhood hardware store and asked the man on duty what kind of paint to use.

The kindly manager, when he discovered I was an amateur, suggested, "Try this paint. It's 'KemTone'—you can use it in any direction. It dries in two to three hours and is only $3.75 a gallon."

On the second day of occupancy, I started to paint the ceiling in the front foyer. Three hours later, I finished. When the front doorbell rang, I scrambled off the stepladder to greet our first guest. Standing before me was an imposing, brown-skinned gentleman with an English accent who intoned,

"I am Mr. Nethersole and my AID (Agency for International Development) adviser gave me this address. May I come in?" His business card stated that he supervised a large banana plantation in Jamaica.

"Of course, but we have a problem—the rooms need to be repainted. We will be ready in a week."

He volunteered, "May I look at one of your guest rooms? Maybe I can paint my own room instead of going back to my solitary confinement in a cheap hotel."

Mr. Nethersole took the remaining KemTone paint, went upstairs and painted the small room he had chosen. Several hours later, he came down and sniffed the aroma of the roast beef I was preparing for dinner.

My husband invited him to dine with us. After dinner, he stayed for a while and then said, "I just want to tell my roommate Dr. Hu of Taiwan what a friendly home I've found in Washington. If you do not mind, I would like to move in tonight." He did.

The next day, Dr. Hu, a Chinese economist, arrived with him. Dr. Hu also painted his own room. All of our initial guests painted their rooms, resulting in a great savings to the budget.

The plumbing needed major repairs during the first month. When Mike, a hard-bitten plumber of Polish descent, learned that we were a non-profit institution devoted to world peace, he donated his services, charging only for the cost of the materials.

The electrical system was completely outdated and the lights often went on and off of their own accord. An electrical contractor also donated his know-how "as unto the Lord" and rewired most of the building when he was apprised of what we were attempting to accomplish for America and for better world relationships.

Shortly after the Easter season, a strong-looking, mature lady carrying only one well-worn suitcase knocked on the door.

She declared, "I am a traveling missionary for God to the United States of America. I heard about your place in Europe. Do you have a room for several weeks for me until God shows me what my next step should be?"

She was very talkative and shared her life experiences with other guests at the dinner table.

A native of Holland, she had been unjustly imprisoned by the Nazis and had amazingly survived a Holocaust concentration camp. Her life seemed to be a string of one miracle after another. We were all enthralled by her phenomenal experiences and how God had sustained her.

Two weeks later, she received a letter and announced, "God has sent me a ticket to California to meet the leaders of the Billy Graham Crusade. The Holy Spirit wants me to move on to the next step. May God bless you all!"

Several years later, we bought a copy of *The Hiding Place* and read most of the stories she had told us at the dinner table and in the sitting room.

Miss Corrie ten Boom had discovered the exact place where God wanted her to be an effective witness for Him!

A renowned Indonesian artist, Mr. Effendi, was fed up with existing in hotels and other places where he felt like a prisoner in a jail with nobody to talk to and no place where he could eat and cook rice and other Asian foods.

He had been steered to the House by a Chinese friend in New York who had previously enjoyed our homestyle atmosphere.

Mr. Effendi cared not for a room and was quite satisfied to have a blanket and a sheet for a bedroll. He slept on the ledge of a large front window in our sitting room. As an early riser, he simply stashed his bed linens in a corner of the office. (Fortunately, no housing inspector appeared during those weeks.) He shared and participated in all the activities as if he had always been a member of the family.

After a month or so, he returned to his homeland. Occasionally, we received progress reports or saw his name or picture in the newspapers.

Our experience with "Maria" forced us to learn how difficult it could be for some people associated with the "Embassy-lifestyle."

She was at the front door long before breakfast, pleading in Spanish that we grant her immediate asylum, having heard that we were kind and loving to strangers. She had escaped from her embassy and the ambassador's home and felt that her life was in danger. If she were caught and returned, she knew she would "disappear."

As a virtual slave, she worked more than a hundred hours per week without pay or any other kind of remuneration. To ensure her servility and obedience, her master retained her passport.

Over the breakfast table, she cried out her life story and times of hardships in the land of freedom—America!

Although there were no empty rooms available, we were able to fix up a large closet space that opened into the Chapel. This ample walk-in closet became her bedroom. We gave her part-time employment while we communicated with the State Department regarding the protocol to solve this untoward situation.

She eventually was able to obtain her passport, learn enough English to obtain a job and to rent a safe room of her own in a neighborhood far from her country's embassy.

At least one Friday evening or Saturday afternoon per month, the House became a center for the residents of the Baltimore-based Flynn Houses for recovering alcoholics.

Mr. Arthur Pratt, world traveler and former resident of the House, moved to Baltimore and began a work among alcoholics. He later headed the Flynn Houses as live-in director and counselor.

As part of the rehabilitation process, he accompanied some of the residents to the House so they could hold a meeting, readjust to the social graces which would enable them to rejoin society and partake of a family atmosphere.

Many years later, when Mr. Pratt returned to his family printing press business in Indiana, he continued with the rehabilitation program of alcoholics and other addicts.

We were honored one week when the U.S.-born man who declared himself to be "World Citizen Number One" stayed with us for several days and wanted "to share the peace" with us and with Washington—if it would listen to peace as a way of life instead of war.

When Dr. Glenn Clark, Board President, visited us in the spring of 1957, staying for a week, he suggested that I give a Dinner for Internationals. He asked me to invite the press attaches of Pakistan and Afghanistan embassies whose countries were then in open warfare with one another.

I hesitated. "That will be impossible for me to do," I smiled. "They are actually at war."

Dr. Clark reiterated, "Just plan your dinner party as I suggested. Invite the two press attaches and let us see what happens afterwards."

It was difficult to say "no" to the President of the Board and a man who was a leading published authority on the effectiveness of prayer.

Following his plan, I invited several embassy officials and Congresswoman Ruth Thompson of Michigan as guest speaker. At the formal seated dinner, all the guests were on time with the exception of the two press attaches of Pakistan and Afghanistan. When the two attaches finally arrived, they had to sit together at the only unoccupied table. Congresswoman Thompson spoke on "Peace in Our Time." The evening was very successful with a question-and-answer forum enjoyed by all. Dr. Clark spent much of his time talking to the two press attaches who were inspired by the speech of the Congresswoman. Both promised to bring back to their embassies their respective impressions.

Many continued in prayer. What a surprise when a week after the dinner, a daily Washington newspaper front page featured a banner headline,

"Pakistan and Afghanistan Are Friends Again!"

Can two Middle East antagonists live together?

Well, we had an amazing surprise! One afternoon, an Egyptian doctor from the United Nations made an unusual appeal. He said he was very homesick and requested me to prepare a home-cooked Egyptian meal.

Twenty-four houseguests from eighteen countries enjoyed the Egyptian dinner. Everybody was relaxed and we were like a big family. After-dinner conversation was so enlivened that we barely heard the doorbell ring.

When my husband opened the door, he saw an Israeli doctor, also on a United Nations assignment from New York, who had a late room reservation! But, we had a problem. The House was full and there was no room for another person.

The only possibility was to "double up," and the only room large enough to accommodate a cot was the Egyptian doctor's room. So while my husband served a late dinner to the newcomer, I asked the Egyptian doctor if he would be kind enough to allow a fellow U.N. doctor to stay on a cot in his room on an emergency basis.

After thoroughly enjoying his Egyptian dinner, he waxed poetical, gesticulating,

"If I could reach that moon shining so brightly outside, I would gladly give it to you for a gift. Whatever you desire, it shall be yours."

Then, and only then, did I dare introduce him to the doctor from Israel. It was a "match"! Both were gregarious types and had similar U.N. grant study assignments. For at least a week, these two men whose countries were enemies saw peace and friendship become reality.

From 1954 to 1958, The House on Nineteenth Street had been host to 110 nations. Our guests included Latin Americans, Caribbeans, Europeans, Africans, Far Easterners and Near Easterners. It was a wonderful feeling to realize that so many different peoples found friendships and lasting goodwill as they stayed under one roof in such a short duration.

All American holidays including Christmas and New Year's Day were special occasions. People from countries who did not have the Christmas tree tradition or even celebrate Christmas experienced the thrill of decorating a large Christmas tree with glistening ornaments and twinkling lights. They also enjoyed the midnight snacks of festive cookies and cakes and Christmas caroling. Our New Year's Eve programs in the Chapel followed by a midnight dinner with special dishes native to their countries were always a time of enthusiasm and good fellowship.

I can testify to the old American proverb, "What goes around comes around."

Eventually, my *own* Philippine Embassy required assistance.

Lifting the telephone receiver one day, I recognized the voice of Mrs. Carlos P. Romulo, the wife of the new ambassador.

"*Cómo está usted?*" Mrs. Romulo inquired. After three minutes of chit-chat following the Filipino custom, she hinted, "We have a tiny problem. Can you, in your kindness, possibly help your fellow countrymen in their time of distress while they are in a distant and foreign land?"

In like manner I replied, "It will be to my utmost happiness

International House Reception at Philippine Embassy (left to right) **Mrs. Block, C.P. Romulo** (Philippine Ambassador to UN), **Mrs. Romualdez, Eduardo Romualdez** (Philippine Ambassador to Washington, DC), **Mariles Cacho Romulo, Ruby Rojas,** (daughter of Manuel Roxas, former President of the Philippines), **Mary O'Neill** (daughter of former American Ambassador to the Philippines)

and honor to be of service to you. In what way may I aid my dear homeland at this present hour?"

Mrs. Romulo commented, "The *Bayanihan*, a Philippine good-will folk dance troupe of thirty young men and women touring and performing in the USA, have lost their financial support.

"Their last performance was in New York City. They are arriving in Washington, D.C., without funding.

"Would you in your kindness and worthiness be able to provide them with room and board for three days, until their management is able to underwrite and reschedule their performance?" Mrs. Romulo requested.

Although I didn't know how we could house that many people with only three hours notice, I assured Mrs. Romulo that they would at least have a roof over their heads and one home-style meal daily.

We doubled up in every room. My family rearranged the library with canvas cots to accommodate the women. The men were

**Mrs. Perle Mesta, Ambassador to Luxembourg, with author
at Philippine Embassy**

assigned bedrolls on the floor of the Chapel and one even slept behind my office desk.

After a coffee and doughnut breakfast, they proceeded to their folklore dance practice on the stage of the downtown Warner Theater.

Each evening I prepared an ample dinner emphasizing Philippine cuisine. Overflowing platters of steamed white rice were devoured by the hungry, athletic participants.

In turn, the *Bayanihan* members entertained our other residents with their Philippine songs. All expenses, especially food, were covered from our own personal resources.

Finally, the group was refinanced, and they proceeded on their American tour.

Several weeks later, at an Embassy party, Mrs. Romulo thanked me.

After a year's directorship we had housed people from almost fifty nations. We inaugurated an Embassy Welcome Party hosting ambassadors of the countries registered in our visitors book.

The guest of honor was the "Dean of the Diplomatic Corps," the Honorable Guillermo Sevilla-Sacasa of Nicaragua.

At ceremonies in the Chapel area, fifteen ambassadors and Charge d'Affaires presented their country's flags in a dedication ceremony in honor of their citizens' participation.

Each ambassador summarized the history and aspirations of his native land.

The flags were received by Mr. Glen Harding, the President of the House on Nineteenth Street and Koinonia Foundation, and displayed in positions of prominence.

As a finale, we sang melodies characteristic to each country, followed by a smorgasbord of national dishes.

This gala occasion proved to be a great boost to the ongoing purpose of the House and to international relations of the countries involved.

When Nicaragua later suffered from a devastating natural disaster, guests and American friends of the House, especially from Greensboro and High Point, North Carolina, pledged funding for the purchase of 10,000 pounds of rice to be distributed to the homeless victims through the cooperation of Ambassador Sevilla-Sacasa.

Later they graciously invited us to the Nicaraguan Embassy for a thank-you reception.

At a subsequent embassy festivity, the former Chairman of the U.S. War Damage Commission to the Philippines took me aside and apologized for not having been able to assist me in my claims for the destruction of *The Commonwealth Advocate* business and offices.

I stressed that I had petitioned the U.S. Government for $124,000 in damages but had received a check for less than $500!

He stammered, "I only wish that I had known you personally then. Things would have been much different. If I had only known then what I know now." He continued, "My hands were tied. There were so many false claimants. Too much politics. I'm sorry."

"John," I responded, "it's too late to cry over spilt milk. We're still friends!"

Arsenio Lacson, recipient of a governmental exchange pro-

Author and the Honorable Mr. Hickerson, American Ambassador to The Philippines at International House Reception

gram, was a House guest for two weeks. Several years later, after he returned to the Philippines, he was overwhelmingly elected mayor of Manila.

When the United States Department of State invited him to participate in the International Conference of Municipal and City Governments in Washington, D.C., he was unable to attend because of political unrest.

Instead, he requested that I attend the Conference in his place as the Acting Mayor of Manila.

Mayor Lacson telegrammed the essential credentials; and I became the Acting Mayor of Manila and had an active part in the program, including the Pathway to Peace and People-to-People Sister Cities.

Upon reflection, it seemed to be a gift of Grace that when one serves humbly, he or she may be recognized by others as worthy of larger things and greater services in due time.

Acting Mayor of Manila, Mrs. Block at United Nations Conference

Acting Mayor of Manila, Mrs. Block with Chairman of UN Conference

Chapter 30

LOVE OVERCOMES REVENGE

One late spring afternoon as I was cultivating pansies with a small trowel in the little garden patch in front of the House, a taxi pulled up. Two gentlemen got out. I instantly recognized one of them! He was the Officer-in-Charge of Fort Santiago torture prison in Manila during the Japanese Occupation of the Philippines. I almost went into a state of shock!

In a flash it all came back to me—my imprisonment there for nearly three months! He was the same officer who interrogated me and ordered my inhumane torture.

I thought, "How did such a 'top name' escape being indicted and brought to justice in the War Crimes trials?

"How or why did the U.S. State Department let him slip through its investigative procedures and not be alerted to his wartime activities? Surely he was a mass-murderer!

"Look at those lips that so easily commanded, 'Pull out her thumb nail! Tie her up for another water treatment!'

"And look at those—eyes that showed so much hatred and anger!

"Those eyes!"

"*Aaaiieeeee*! This is my chance for revenge," I internalized. "I'll take this trowel and jab it into those cruel eyes. He *MUST* pay for what he did to me!"

In that exact moment of indignation, anger, revulsion, some unexplained Power, beyond my comprehension, forced the trowel to drop from my hand. Clunk!

And instead, calmly, I walked slowly forward to welcome them in their own language. I showed them to their rooms and introduced them to my family. The inquisitor showed no recognition at all. That night I cooked them a Japanese specialty, *Sukiyaki*, for dinner.

The third night of their stay, seated at the dinner table with eighteen different nationalities present, Mr. Nishimura, in his broken English asked my husband, "Where were you during—war? Your wife—Philippine—yes?"

Instead, I answered him, "I was in Fort Santiago Prison for three months."

There was a long—long silence. He arose, faced my husband and spoke again in broken English, "Me—no good. I—no live here, because I was bad to your wife and people—Philippine. Me—go!"

My husband tapped him on the shoulder and said, "This is a home inspired by God's love, established to promote Peace and Love among peoples of the world. You are most welcome here."

Mr. Nishimura and his friend stayed with us for three weeks. In that short time, he daily questioned, "What make people—like you—love others?"

No Japanese male ever helps in the kitchen, but he was constantly by my side assisting me as I washed and dried dishes. He queried me again and again as to why I could serve him food and not seek revenge.

We tried to explain to him that the Lord who was the Prince of Peace makes it possible for people to love one another instead of filling their hearts with hatred and war. Also, that His very presence in our daily lives can make that difference.

Mr. Nishimura wanted to know the Prince of Peace, so he went to a local drugstore and bought a *New Testament*. He studied it without ceasing.

Several days later he announced that he knew the Prince of Peace and was now a "changed" man!

We gained a lifelong friend, and to this day retain a friendship with him and his family in Japan.

I thought that after this experience, I had finally attained "clo-

Mrs. Block with Gen. Wainwright. Photo was taken at the National Convention of the Disabled Veterans Legion in Washington, D.C. in 1949. The two met in Bataan when then Mrs. Blanco was covering the war front for her husband's magazine, the Commonwealth Advocate.

A FILIPINA

By BETTY SCHNELL
KISLAP-*graphic* Washington Bureau

ta Block who, during all these struggles, stayed braved and confident, a feeling sustained greatly by the help and sympathy of her equally brave second husband Isaac Block whom she met and married in the Philippines in 1945.

Still In Washington, D.C.

Since then so many have wondered what happened to this guerrilla heroine and knowing that she is still residing in Washington D.C., I made inquiries and got her address. When I called on her, naturally our conversation, after the usual amenities, turned to her 1948 mission in behalf of Philippine guerrilla veterans.

As she poured tea for me this

war heroine who is sligh and hardly five feet tal of the hard times that she husband Isaac went throu completion of the mission recalled with extreme vivid action that the Philippine ment had taken against refusing her more funda able to return home when ready and what she had after this to bring to the her sons Florentino and Pet cumstances, been separat three years. She told touching answer of many people and friends to her for her own and interested Sen. Kennett (R-Neb.) who helped sec boys' entry into the United

MANILANS may well remember that in the year 1948 a Manila paper carried the shocking story of a Filipino war widow and guerrilla heroine who unfolded before American high-ranking officials in Washington, D.C. a story of brazen graft and corruption in the Philippines involving millions of American dollars. This war widow, who was sent to the United States by Philippine veterans to plead for additional money for unrecognized guerrillas in the islands, had charge that the millions intended for these men was detoured somewhere along the way between Washington, D.C. and Manila and that instead of reaching deserving veterans or their kin, the money landed in the pockets of certain politicians.

A Woman's Victory

The charges were indeed serious and top Philippine officials tried to stop what the erring politicians had termed "washing of dirty linen in public" by this widow and we, have must immediate return a extent that the But convinced of justice must [...] for some-

by the fact that she had a "bagful of documentary proof" to back her charges, the war widow and heroine remained calm and steady and refused to go home. This started off Uncle Sam's investigations of the case. The heroine's proof was exhibited. After a series of investigations and hearings of the case, as if in answer to the widow's plea for help for compatriots back home, another huge sum was approved by the American government for World War II Philippine veterans.

This was more than a personal victory for Mamerta Block, the guerrilla heroine and widow of the late Pedro Blanco, editor of the *Commonwealth Advocate*. To her it was a great victory for a great cause, and naturally it brought her happiness, a happiness however that was destined to be short-lived for after that one victory came other struggles she had to face. These were her efforts to obtain visas to the U.S. for her two sons by her first marriage; for financial assistance; for survival in a strange country; for security. All this however ended well for Mamer-

Mrs. Block poses with American Congresswoman [...] when the latter gave a luncheon in honor of Mrs. Block [...]

In photo at top left Mrs. Block again greets Gen. Wainwright—seven years after the Battle of Bataan.

sure" to my wartime suffering. Twenty years later on a trip to Manila, we visited Fort Santiago as tourists. However, we were not allowed to enter the area of detention cells. The very sight and then the sensation of walking through the halls brought forth too many memories of the horrific groanings and screamings of the torture victims.

It was an emotional crisis for me. I ran from the dank and dark interior; through the doorway and into the bright sunlight. My husband embraced me and I cried bitter tears of pain; and, then of release and thanksgiving.

Australian tourists passing by turned their faces in sympathy as my husband explained, "She was once a prisoner here."

The next day we visited Corregidor and observed the ruins and how Japanese tourists lighted memorial candles for their deceased relatives of World War II. I wondered how they would feel if they knew that some of their loved ones had been dissolved into cement and were part of the road they walked on or were imbedded in the structures of public buildings.

Finally, we stopped at the mammoth Peace Memorial.

Standing quietly in the shadow of the gigantic modernistic angel, I gazed over to the Bataan side of the Manila Bay and reminisced of what had transpired almost forty years before. Surveying countless *acres* of white Stars of David and Christian crosses glistening in the blinding tropical sunlight, my eyes gradually focused on the inscription of the nearest cross:

SUGGS—a young Marine from North Carolina who perished in the Battle of the Liberation. And J—from California—where did he die so violently? Who were his parents? S—from Arizona—was he a member of the National Guard called to active duty in early 1941 and sent overseas to protect the Philippines—and trapped in Bataan?

It was difficult to comprehend that each marker covered a once living, breathing, feeling, emotional personality—beloved of somebody back in the United States—and nobody able to visit his final resting place! I wondered if the authorities had at least photographed the grave site and sent a picture to their survivors.

Manila American Cemetery, Republic of Philippines

"The heavy weight of hours has chained and bowed me." It was very disheartening. I thought of another anguished prisoner—"of Chillon." Images of a smiling "Manoling" (President Quezon) tangoing with his wife Aurora amidst the gaiety of the weekly Presidential balls and dances flashed across my mind. So many of them—also dead! But I was still alive and left to continue with my own earthly tasks in the Philippines and the U.S.A.

Somehow or other, I found myself on my knees with hands outstretched upward in supplication. Unsteadily, I arose. Striding over to the inscriptions I recalled that my friend, the Chairman of the Corregidor-Bataan Memorial, the Honorable Emmet O'Neal, former Senator from Kentucky and Ambassador to the Philippines, had also died before the memorial was dedicated on June 22, 1968.

How proud his wife and two daughters had been as they saw the progress of the monument and confided in me their sorrow that he did not live to see its completion.

I reflected upon the wise adage, "Peace is sweeter to those who have known the true meaning of war."

The simple inscription of N.E. Graham was true to me, "No traveler who comes here sees the magnificent monument and stands unawed."

The raised circular altar implores:

"Sleep my sons, your duty done For Freedom's light has come

Sleep in the silent depths of the sea or in your bed of hallowed soil

Until you hear at dawn the low, clear reveille of God"

And yet, I still have occasional flashbacks of torture and sudden deaths of loved ones. It is only God's love that can heal.

"Charity (love)

Beareth all things, Believeth all things,

Hopeth all things, Endureth all things.

Charity never faileth."   (*I Corinthians 13*)

**Eternal Light War Memorial
on the island of Corregidor**

GLOSSARY

Adobo   Meat and/or chicken sautéed with vinegar, garlic and other spices. Usually boiled, never fried.

Banca (Banka)   Native dugout canoe 10-15 feet long; 1-5 oarsmen.

Bibingka   Delicious flat rice cake with sweet coconut topping.

Ca-no (Ka-no)   Abbreviated version of "Americano." Became "code name" for Americans in hiding.

Caratela   Horsedrawn high-wheeled carriage. Especially suited for rainy season and muddy roads. Baggage rack in rear.

Flan   Semi-sweet egg yolk custard. Topped with caramel sauce.

Fort Santiago   MacArthur's Headquarters in Walled City of Intramuros. Site of Japanese torture prison.

Ilustrado   Philippine elite during Spanish Colonial Period.

Intramuros   Old Walled City founded in 1571. Walls were 25 feet high and 40 feet thick. Final center of Japanese resistance in Manila in 1945.

Kempeitai   Japanese Secret Police. Usually compared to Hitler's Gestapo.

Lechon   Young "milk" pig spit-barbecued slowly over hot coals. National delicacy for birthdays, social occasions and religious holidays.

Makapili   Armed collaborators, sympathetic to the Japanese cause. Mostly anti-American.

Malacanan(g)   The Presidential Palace. Philippine
      equivalent of the United States' White House.

Negritos   An aëta-related aborigine usually under five
      feet tall. Member of Negroid race of possible
      Papuan origin. Very muscular. Extremely loyal to
      Americans.

Pancit   Satisfying meal of thin rice noodles mixed with
      shrimp and/or chicken.

"Sus!"   Religious and social exhortation of Grace.
      Abbreviated equivalent to "Jesus! Mary! And
      Joseph!" Usually said simultaneously as
      "JesusMariaJoseph!"

Tagalog   Belongs to Malay-Polynesian language family. Is
      now basis for Pilipino – the new national language.

The Commonwealth Advocate   Monthly family magazine in
      forefront of campaign to continue Commonwealth
      (dominion) status beyond 1946.

Zona! Zona!   Japanese military structured event to isolate
      neighborhood areas in a street-by-street search for
      victims.

PHILIPPINE CONFECTIONS
(Traditional Style)

BIBINGKA

Wash two cups rice; then soak rice in two cups fresh water for at least six hours. (Use older rice. Newly harvested rice does not give good results.) Drop by spoonfuls into a stone grinder and grind. Add water gradually. (This ground mixture is called "galapong.")

    2 cups rice "galapong"
    3 eggs well beaten
    1 cup fresh milk
    2 teaspoons baking powder
    ¾ cup granulated sugar
    Banana leaves (as needed)

Mix the first five ingredients together. Set aside. Soften the banana leaves by passing them over an open flame. Before baking, cut circular-shaped banana leaves to fit clay baking pan which has been pre-heated over a clay stove. Pour one cup of mixture into an 8-inch diameter clay pan. If baking pan is bigger, pour more of the mixture. Arrange strips of yellow cheese on top. Cover with galvanized iron lid. Bake at 250°F until golden brown. Brush top with melted butter. Serve with grated coconut.

PÚTÔ

    2 cups rice "galapong"
    ¾ cup granulated sugar
    2 teaspoons baking powder

Thoroughly mix sugar and "galapong." Add baking powder. Arrange 1½" circular pútô molds on bamboo steamer. Boil water in a deep native saucepan. Set bamboo steamer over the saucepan. Cover with a tight-fitting lid. Steam for 20-30 minutes. Remove steamer from saucepan. Cool and remove from molds. Serve with grated coconut.

KUCHINTA

> 1 cup rice "galapong"
> 1 cup water
> ¾ cup brown sugar
> ½ teaspoon ash-lye solution
> (or ¼ teaspoon sodium bicarbonate)

Mix all ingredients together. Cook like "Pútô."

MAJA BLANCA

> 3 cups grated young corn, or scraped from the cob
> 2 cups rice "galapong"
> 4 cups coconut milk
> 3 cups sugar

Mix the coconut milk, rice "galapong" and corn. Strain through coarse muslin cloth. Add sugar. Boil all ingredients together, stirring constantly until thickened. Pour into greased molds. Allow to cool and slice. Serve with "latik"* and caramelized coconut meal.

For Modern Kitchens:
Use powdered rice from oriental market for "galapong."
Instead of banana leaves, spray PAM on bottom and sides of pan. Also, may use brown paper.
Substitute sodium bicarbonate for ash-lye.
Substitute mini-muffin pan for "pútô" molds.

NOTE: Caloric equivalents were not calculated.

---

* Latik is residue of boiled coconut juice.

SELECTED READINGS

Blanco, Pedro. *The Commonwealth Advocate.* Manila

Blanco, Pedro. *The Phillipine Problem.* Manila, 1933

de los Reyes, Mamerta. *Sulu In Its True Light.* Manila

Elliot, Charles B. *The Philippines to the End of the Military Regime.* Indianapolis, 1917

Kennan, George F. *American Diplomacy, Expanded Edition.* The University of Chicago, Chicago, 1984

Morison, Samuel Eliot. *The Liberation of the Philippines: Luzon, Mindanao, the Visayas, 1944-45.* Little Brown and Co., Boston, 1959

Malay, Armando J. *Occupied Philippines.* Manila, 1967

Manchester, William. *American Caesar.* Little Brown and Co., Boston, 1978

Ten Boom, Corrie. *The Hiding Place.* Chosen Books, Washington Depot, Conn., 1971

Seagrave, Sterling. *The Marcos Dynasty.* Harper & Row, New York, 1988

Willoughby, Charles A. *The Guerilla Resistance Movement in the Philippines.* New York, 1972

Wolfert, Ira. *American Guerilla in the Philippines.* New York, 1945

INDEX